Love
Pattern & Colour

Love Pattern & Colour

THE ESSENTIAL GUIDE

Charlotte Abrahams

FRANCES LINCOLN

Brimming with creative inspiration, how-to projects and useful information to enrich your everyday life, Quarto Knows is a favourite destination for those pursuing their interests and passions. Visit our site and dig deeper with our books into your area of interest: Quarto Creates, Quarto Cooks, Quarto Homes, Quarto Lives, Quarto Drives, Quarto Explores, Quarto Gifts, or Quarto Kids.

First published in 2021 by Frances Lincoln Publishing,
an imprint of The Quarto Group.
The Old Brewery, 6 Blundell Street
London, N7 9BH,
United Kingdom
T (0)20 7700 6700
www.QuartoKnows.com

A catalogue record for this book is available from the British Library.

ISBN 978 0 7112 5748 1
Ebook ISBN 978 0 7112 5749 8

10 9 8 7 6 5 4 3 2 1

Design by Studio Noel
Picture Research by Jane Smith Media

Printed in China

MIX
Paper from
responsible sources
FSC® C016973

CONTENTS

INTRODUCTION

I am not a maker of patterns, but pattern has certainly helped to make me. My earliest memory is a pattern – a repeat print of a pink cat and a white mouse, which wrapped the walls of my first bedroom. I don't remember the room itself, or the house it was in, but the pattern sits in my head. An image of home.

Then there's the blue gingham check of my nursery school art apron; the needle-thin stripes – red, yellow, blue, white – of my favourite jeans; the flower and trellis wallpaper border of my parents' dining room; and the blue-and-white willow print beneath slices of roast chicken at my grandparents' house.

When I first set up home in the mid-1990s, pattern was out of fashion. I was a design writer, a person supposedly in tune with interior trends, so I tried to embrace the plain and the minimal, but I felt ill at ease in my patternless house. Without a pop of print to attract my attention, my eye had nowhere to go, nothing to focus on; plain walls, plain floors and plain furnishings left me feeling as flat as the rooms themselves. Without pattern, there was no depth, no movement, no standout feature and, above all, no joy.

Perhaps I was doing it wrong. I know plain can be interesting but unless it is offsetting pattern, it doesn't interest me. And that's why I'm writing this book. I love pattern and I want you to love it too. More than that, I want you to bring it into your home and make it part of your life because I believe that living with pattern is good for us. It lifts our spirits. It also makes up for all manner of architectural imperfections and is brilliant at hiding domestic detritus from dust to dog hair. Cheering and practical, what's not to love?

But how do you live with pattern? How do you choose? Are you blousy flowers or chic pinstripes, Baroque damask or carefree polka dots, pastoral toile de Jouy or urban geometry? And once you have found your style, how do you bring it into your home?

This book aims to help you find the answers to all those questions. It doesn't set out rules – this is home decoration, there aren't any rules – but it does explain how pattern affects spaces, how light and colour change the way we perceive pattern and how pattern can be used to achieve certain looks. It also offers suggestions on where to look for ideas and, most important of all, contains pages and pages of photographs of gloriously patterned interiors to inspire you. They are a feast for the eyes. Enjoy.

Design: Susi Bellamy.

THE POWER
OF PATTERN

A pattern is created when one or more motifs are repeated at regular – or irregular – intervals. Reduced to such a basic description, pattern sounds simple, dull even, but we all know that pattern is neither of those things. Pattern is complex and invigorating. It delights our eye, lifts our spirits, and orders and ornaments our surroundings.

In our homes, pattern has the power to transform spaces by changing the way we perceive scale. Vertical stripes make a low-ceilinged room appear taller, for example, while a regular repeat print will bring a sense of cohesion to a disjointed open-plan interior. Pattern can also define surfaces, convey a design style and camouflage imperfections. Lumpy plaster on the walls? No problem, a dense floral print will seem to smooth away those bumps. And most important of all, pattern can change the way we feel.

Human beings recognize pattern instinctively. Chaos unsettles us, so we are hard-wired to find patterns to help us organize and make sense of the world. And we are richly rewarded because pattern is everywhere, part of the very structure of nature, from the radial symmetry of snowflakes and sunflowers, to the spirals of a nautilus shell and the hexagonal repeat of honeycomb.

We are also programmed to respond to pattern. Scientific research has shown that we have neurons in our brains that react to lines, edges and bars and that our visual development relies on these neurons being stimulated by exposure to pattern when we are babies. Even as adults, our eyes are on a constant quest for visual arousal. A study looking into adults' emotional response to pattern, carried out by George Stylios, Senior Research Professor at Heriot-Watt University, and research student Meixuan Chen, revealed that the participants on the trial registered more excitement when they were shown intense patterns rather than weak ones, and more pleasure when they were shown repeating patterns rather than non-repeats.

No wonder then that we have been making pattern part of our homes for as long as we have had places to call home. Patterns have been found in prehistoric cave paintings; Ancient Egyptians wove rushes into patterns to form decorative wall hangings and floor coverings; and, when the Pueblo Indians began to settle rather than roam, around 500CE, they took to decorating their clay pots with patterns composed of geometric, floral and animal motifs. Roll forward to the Victorian age and we find pattern rioting through homes large and small. The Victorians may have a reputation for domestic prudery, but they embraced interior pattern with joyous abandon. Lace curtains hung beside fleur-de-lis wallpaper, and chairs wrapped in floral upholstery sat proudly on garlanded carpets.

There have been attempts to drive pattern off our walls, floors and furnishings. In 1908, the Austrian architect Alfred Loos published a pamphlet entitled 'Ornamentation and Crime', which stated that decoration had no place in the new, rational, machine-driven century. Eighty-eight years later, the Swedish furniture giant IKEA released a television advertising campaign that urged its British customers to 'chuck out the chintz'.

These exhortations did indeed change tastes – the architects and designers behind both the Modern Movement and the Bauhaus were heavily influenced by Loos' ideas, while IKEA's attack on floral prints helped to usher in a decade of neutral-toned minimalism – but not for long. Pattern-free moments have always been short-lived because, without it, our homes bring us neither excitement nor pleasure and a home without these is no home at all.

Opposite: With its fresh blue, white and yellow colour scheme, this pretty, pattern-filled kitchen speaks of carefree summer days. However, there is nothing casual about how the multiple layers of geometric patterns have been brought together – and that's why the scheme works. Look closely and you'll see that the straight lines that anchor the wall tiles in the foreground are echoed in the simple squares on the back kitchen wall and the chevrons on the wooden shutters.

FINDING INSPIRATION & GATHERING TREASURE

Interior designers are magpies, constantly on the lookout for treasure to gather up and take home. And like magpies, their notion of treasure covers all manner of seemingly mundane and unremarkable objects – a dropped button, a discarded wrapper, a fallen berry – because what they are drawn to is not the thing itself, but rather its colour, or texture, or pattern. This is where inspiration comes from.

Being attentive to what attracts you as you live in the world is probably the most important trick of the interior design trade because it teaches you about your own taste. I discovered that I have a thing for stripes and shades of grey when, in a pre-move clear out, I collected up all my old coats and found each of the pockets contained a striped stone or two, picked up on beach walks and instantly forgotten. Looking at them all together made me realize that the patterns and colours on these stones are a constant theme in both my home and my wardrobe and that they bring me real joy.

Joy should be the starting point for every home decorating project, regardless of scale. Once the functional stuff is dealt with – the boiler, the washing machine, the kids' toys etc. – the rest is ornamentation, so it must speak to your aesthetic. Start channelling your inner interior designer/magpie with a collection of treasures. Simply open your eyes next time you go out and notice the things you like. Pick them up or take a snap on your phone and before long you will find you have amassed a miscellany of stuff that delights your eye.

The next step is to go through it and identify recurring colours, patterns and textures. These are things you are naturally drawn to and should therefore be the foundation of your interior scheme.

Now you have your basic palette, you can start thinking about how to make it work in a room. Another trick of the trade is to make a mood board. Used by interior designers to present prospective schemes to their clients, these collages are also a brilliant way to help home decorators define ideas and test out different looks. There are lots of apps to help you create digital versions, but physical ones work best because they give you a more accurate sense of colours and a feel for the textures too.

Making a mood board is easy:

1. Find a large (A3) piece of thick card and some masking tape.
2. Gather together all the elements you are considering using in the scheme. Images torn from magazines, photographs, paint samples (buy a tester pot and paint a piece of paper rather than relying on a printed colour chart), swatches of fabric and wallpaper.
3. Find some drawing pins, masking tape or other easy-to-remove adhesive (you want to be able to move all the elements around) and start creating your board. Begin with the piece you want to build the scheme around – if it's something you already own such as a sofa, take a photograph of it and print it out so you can see how it works with everything else. Think about the scale too – if you are considering covering all the walls in a particular wallpaper, then make that the biggest sample on the board.
4. Now start adding accents and accessories. Play around with different colours, patterns and textures to see what works. You might need to make several boards.
5. Place the board (or boards) in the room you are planning to decorate and live with it for a while. Look at how the light changes through the day and how that affects the colours.

All this takes time but it really is worth the investment. And it's good fun too.

DEFINING YOUR
OWN STYLE

Picking out patterns you love is just the start of the story; now you have to decide how you are going to use them to create an environment that complements your existing decor and furniture, works with your lifestyle, reflects your personality and, most important of all, makes you feel at home.

The following pages show the range of different styles you can create with pattern. Divided into five broad looks – Serene & Simple; Opulent Glamour; Pop Bright; Urban Chic; and Contemporary Classic – they are designed to demonstrate the versatility of pattern and help you to identify an overall mood. These themes are not definitive and, while you might instantly relate to one, you are equally likely to find that there are elements that speak to you in each of them. That's fine, a dash of Pop Bright would look great in a Serene & Simple living space; this is all about finding out what you like – and, equally importantly, what you don't. Take time to really examine each image, noting the patterns, colours and combinations that you are naturally drawn to. Then look at your mood boards and collection of treasures. Where are the crossovers?

Now look at the room you are planning to decorate. Does it share any characteristics with your favourite image? If not, you might want to think again. Pattern can be transformative, but it can't turn a long, narrow Victorian sitting room into a glass-fronted, twenty-first century living/eating zone. Think too about what the space is used for. A serene scheme of pale-on-pale patterns might work in a grown-up bedroom, but it's probably not the best choice for a family kitchen. The most successful and satisfying interiors are those that are both beautiful and fit for purpose.

Once you have pinpointed the general mood you are aiming to create, you can start turning it into a reality. Order wallpaper and fabric samples, stick them on the walls, wrap them round chairs and cushions and live with them a while. How do they work together? How does the light in the room change the way you see them through the day? What happens when you start introducing patterned objects such as vases, lampshades, tableware and rugs? Don't rush this stage; you need time to experiment and move things around. When you walk into the room and feel good then you know you have got it right.

Right and Opposite: Two sitting rooms, both filled with layers of pattern but with very different results – proof that there really is a pattern scheme for everyone. In the minimal black-and-white room, the geometric wallpaper not only provides the scheme's central pattern, it also adds texture, preventing the space from feeling too stark. The maximal scheme on the facing page owes its coherence to those subtle, but repeated, flashes of blue. Right: Design: Arte. Opposite: Design: Kirill Istomin.

SERENE & SIMPLE

If you thought patterned interiors were all about pulse-raising prints and high-octane colours, think again. Pattern-filled rooms can be every bit as soothing to live in as their plain cousins. And much more interesting.

Right: This calm and inviting living space is a glorious melange of textural pattern. A feature wall composed of four tiled panels, each quarter bearing a different geometric pattern, takes centre stage, but rather than let it stand alone as the only patterned element in a plain scheme, it has been combined with four other layers of graphic pattern. There's the abstract printed pattern on the cushions, the stripes of the metal cladding on the wall and ceiling, the inlay on the wooden furniture and artwork and the weave of the pendant lampshade. Bringing all these different patterns together lessens the impact of the feature wall, resulting in a wonderfully harmonious scheme. The warm, earth-toned colours add to the overall effect.
Design: Daniel Heath Studio.

Above: Using an exposed brick wall is a clever way to introduce pattern, as well as texture and colour, into a minimal interior.

Opposite: Both the wall and the curtains carry pattern in this bedroom, but the pale colours, spare, linear forms and nature-inspired theme create a calm and suitably restful mood.

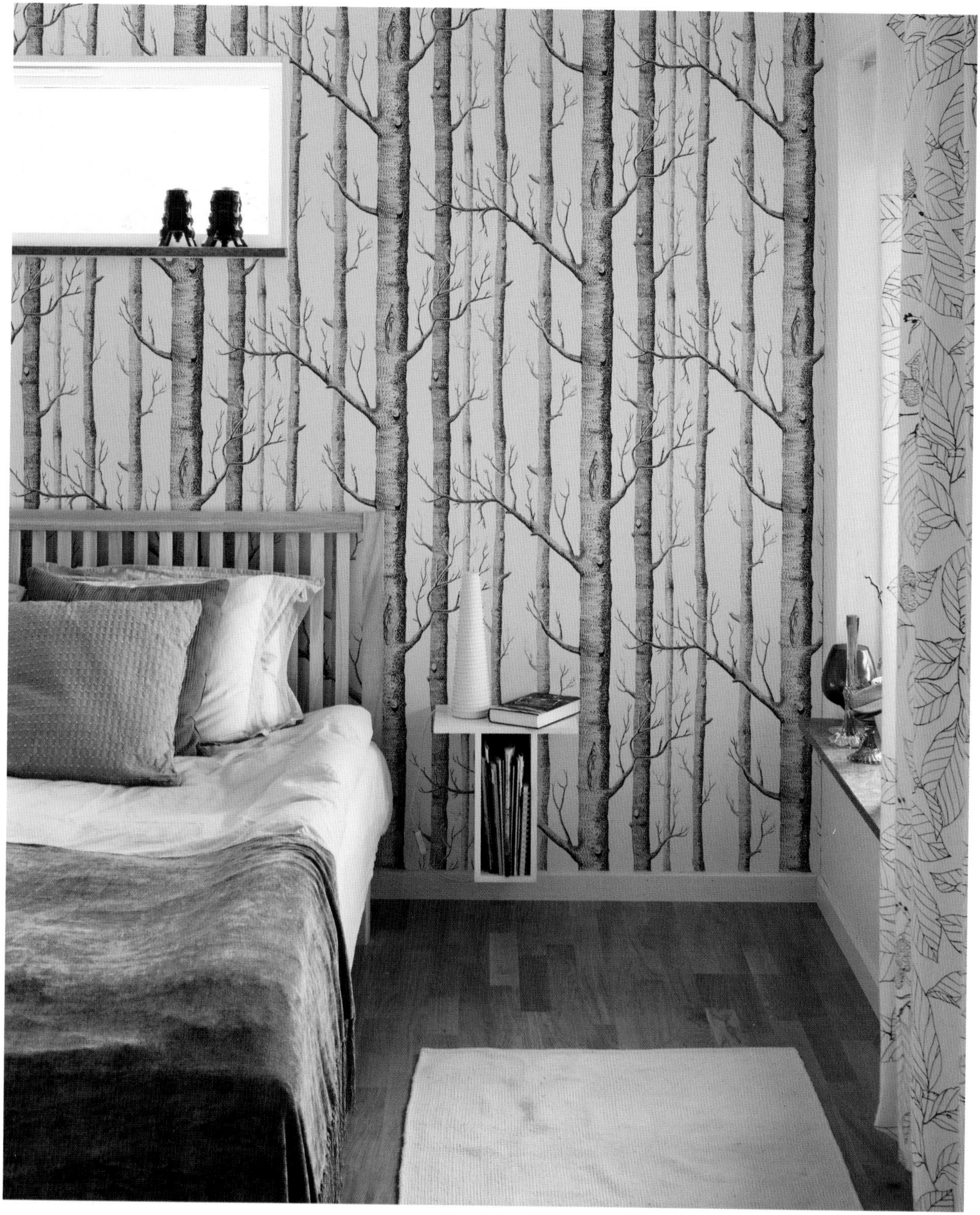

OPULENT GLAMOUR

Glamour and opulence are back in fashion. More is more with this look (interior designers don't call it maximalism for nothing), so think layers of lavish pattern, jewel colours and plenty of shine.

Above: A single pattern used over several different applications – in this case, the walls, cushions, pouffe and lampshade – is a clever way to fill a room with pattern without overloading the senses. Using that pattern in a palette of rich, jewel colours and mixing it with luxurious, sheen-filled fabrics creates a fabulous feeling of opulence.
Design: Susi Bellamy.

Opposite: In this super-luxe living room, the star attraction is the marble-like pattern covering the back wall, the painterly splodges and marks of which bring a lovely sense of movement to the space. The other pattern elements come from the sofa, floor and ceiling. Each is patterned differently but they are linked by their shared geometry. The formality of these patterns acts as an anchor for that fluid feature wall.

Opposite: Hallways and landings make perfect canvases for sumptuous pattern because they are spaces you pass through, rather than live in. The vibrant red wallpaper with its tight-repeat leaf motif pattern makes this landing fizz with energy, but the scheme's sense of depth and opulent elegance is a result of the clever layering of other patterns. The rectangular drawers on the chest are outlined in slightly curved white lines, echoing the geometry of the wallpaper, while the floral print on the ottoman picks up on the botanical theme of the central motif and brings some fluid movement to the space. The large mirror reflecting the abstract geometric print of the study curtains introduces yet another layer of interest.
Design: Kirill Istomin.

Above Left: Decorating two connecting rooms in contrasting patterns is a good way to get the maximal look without visual overload. Leave the door open and you have an extravagant pattern clash; close it and you are left to enjoy the power of the single, wraparound print. In this scheme, a pair of burnt-orange velvet stools in the green room reflect the colour of the walls next door, neatly linking the two spaces together.
Design: Susi Bellamy.

Above Right: Pattern combining doesn't come much more magnificent than this. The effect is certainly bold and bright, but there is a sense of cohesion too because all but one of the – many – patterns used has its root in that simplest of motifs, the straight line.
Design: Kirill Istomin.

URBAN CHIC

This is the sophisticated, metropolitan face of patterned living. And you don't have to live in the city to make it your own. Stripes and geometrics are a fast route to simple, urban elegance, or try pretty motifs such as botanical patterns in a monochrome palette.

Left: The pattern notes are subtle in this grand and grown-up living room, but they are also essential to the success of the scheme. Without the geometric prints on the cushions, the exposed brick wall and those scrolling motifs on the ceiling cornices, it would be a very flat space indeed.

Above: Animal prints can be kitsch but they can also be very smart indeed, particularly when they are combined with traditional furniture. This is an eclectic scheme and the juxtaposition of the leopard print against the floral rug is brave (it goes against the accepted guidelines around combining pattern because the scales of the motif on each are similar, while the colours come from different palettes), but the plain, dark grey wall provides an anchoring framework. The slightly larger scale motifs on the sofa cushions, as well as their black and red colours, also help to pull the scheme together.
Design: Lisa Gilmore Design.

Opposite: Few spaces respond to an injection of high design more readily than tiny cloakrooms and few things say urban chic more clearly than dark colours and repeated geometric shapes.

POP BRIGHT

Add vivid colour to pattern and you instantly raise its tempo. Used as an energizing accent, or taken wall-to-wall, hot colour and pattern are a bold, bright and very beautiful combination.

Above: In this sitting room, pop-bright pattern is just that, a pop of brightness and pattern in an otherwise white room. And it makes the space sing.

Opposite: This is patterned living at its brightest and most playful. There is a lot going on, but the effect is surprisingly harmonious because each pattern and colour is echoed somewhere else in the room. The circles on the rug, for example, are reflected in the swirling shapes on the sofa and the mirrors on the back wall, while the yellow and blue squares on the storage unit find their match in the plain cushions.
Design: Kirill Istomin.

Opposite: There are three layers of bold geometric pattern in this small dining space: stripes, circles and squares. Separated by blocks of plain colour, each stands as a feature in its own right, but they also balance each other in terms of scale and intensity of colour, which means the room comes together as a cohesive scheme.

Above: This sugar-bright sitting/dining room shows how adding a single pattern element can pull a scheme together. Here, the white stripes in the matching pair of sofas draw attention to the window frames in the dining area, providing a visual connection between the two spaces.

CONTEMPORARY CLASSIC

This look is all about taking classic patterns such as damask, roses and chinoiserie and using them in a totally twenty-first century way to create interiors you will want to live with for years to come.

Right: Here, a traditional chinoiserie pattern has been paired with elegant furniture covered in plain velvet upholstery that reflects the colours used in the wallpaper. The effect is both utterly modern and totally timeless.
Design: Graham & Brown.

Opposite: As in the previous scheme, the contemporary classic mood of this bedroom comes as much from the furniture (the ornate headboard conjures up thoughts of eighteenth-century France) as the pattern. The romantic, photo-real floral wallpaper is offset by the sharper edges of the graphic motifs on the bedspread and blanket.
Design: Kirill Istomin.

Above: The rug and curtains are the traditional pattern elements in this richly layered living room and act as a framework for the other, more contemporary motifs. The style of the furniture adds to the traditional feel – the same patterns used with more pared-back, modern furniture would have resulted in a scheme that was more pop bright than contemporary classic.
Design: Kirill Istomin.

USING PATTERN

Decorating is like cooking; success depends on an understanding of the raw ingredients so, before you begin, take a long look at the room you are planning to fill – or least sprinkle – with pattern. Where does the light fall? What architectural features (cornices, skirting boards, fireplaces, beams etc.) do you have? Where is the focal point? Not everything may be as you would wish – you may have low ceilings, too little light or a featureless open-plan kitchen – but as you will discover on the following pages, there are pattern solutions to almost all of these problems.

Once you have a clear idea of the physical space, ask yourself what you want to achieve. Pattern can be used to draw attention to a specific place or feature, it can be used to create flow and continuity across a large area and it can alter our perception of scale. Patterns with three-dimensional effects such as trellises or landscapes, for example, will make a room appear bigger, vertical stripes will seem to raise a low ceiling and a rhythmic repeat will add a sense of depth.

Motif is the starting point for all pattern, but the thing that gives it its impact is the way that motif covers the background and how it's arranged across the surface of the material on which it is used. Known as the 'repeat', it provides a path for our eye to follow, creating a sense of rhythm. An 'open' repeat, where the motifs are spread out across the background, has a gentle, flowing rhythm that will bring a sense of calm to a room, while the tightly placed motifs of a 'closed' repeat speed up our eye movements, raising the tempo of the surrounding space.

Scale, which is the size of the pattern in relation to the room, also has an effect. Large-scale patterns will help to pull a space together, while smaller patterns are a good way to draw attention to a specific area such as a fireplace wall.

Received wisdom has it that both the scale of the pattern and the size of the repeat should increase with the size of the room. In other words, small rooms should be decorated with small, closed-repeat patterns and large rooms with large, open ones. This is a good rule of thumb, but it is worth noting that, when it comes to scale, the reverse can also be true: a tiny pattern used across a large space, for example, can be very effective as we perceive it less as pattern and more as colour and texture. Conversely, a large-scale pattern used wall-to-wall in a small room, such as a cloakroom, adds a wonderful sense of drama.

Using a single pattern in a single place is straightforward – simply choose a design that makes your soul sing, consider the scale and repeat and go for it. However, if you are planning a multi-patterned room then you need to be aware of how different patterns work together.

There are five basic guidelines for mixing patterns:
1. Vary the scale so you don't have too many patterns competing for attention. Aim for a large primary design mixed with smaller-scale accent patterns.
2. Stick to a colour palette across the scheme – or go for contrast. If you choose the latter option, choose shades from opposite sides of the colour wheel.
3. Find a family resemblance, such as natural textures, country of origin or motif theme (floral, geometric etc.), to bring the look together.
4. Go for odd numbers of patterns – three, or five if you are feeling brave.
5. Add some plains to give the patterns space to breathe. A 60/40 pattern-to-plain ratio is about right.

If you are new to patterned living, try mixing in a small way first. Heap some differently patterned cushions on your sofa, or try setting the table with a mix of floral and geometric tableware and see how you like it. When you do decide to take the pattern look wall-to-wall (which you will!), remember to scatter the patterns right across the room, rather than heaping them in one area. If you have a patterned feature wall on one side, for example, place a patterned rug or chair on the other to create a sense of balance.

Clockwise: Design: Arte. Design: Osborne & Little. Design: Mark Alexander. Design: Amelia Graham.

COLOUR & PATTERN

Colour and pattern are often treated as separate ways of introducing drama and interest to our homes. And they do, of course, but they are also intricately related, each altering the mood and our perceptions of the other. For example, a high-energy closed repeat rendered in a gentle shade of cream or grey becomes calming and quiet, while a soothing, open repeat of floral sprigs will burst into life if the flowers are turned vivid red.

Colour also plays a vital role when it comes to mixing patterns in a room. The guidelines are just the same as they are for combining solid colours. Start by using your gathered treasures to choose a main palette. This will be your dominant colour so let instinct be your guide here and choose the one that lifts your spirits. Then look around the colour wheel for the supporting and accent colours. The colours you choose will be dictated by the mood you are trying to create – if you're after something bold, opt for colours from the opposite side of the wheel such as blue and orange, but if serene is the end goal, choose colours that sit next to each other like red, orange and yellow.

Many patterns are themselves made up of several colours and this again affects the impact they have on a space. Colour combinations based on various shades and tones of the same colour are subtle and calming. However, viewed from a distance they can be rather dull so use them in places where you can appreciate the delicate variations – perhaps a pale pink spotted cushion on an armchair upholstered in dark pink stripes.

Complex patterns featuring several contrasting colours have the opposite effect, bringing energy and drama to an interior. Used on a single cushion, vase or lampshade, busy patterns will make a scheme pop, but they need space if used on the wall. It might sound counter-intuitive, but the larger the area, the more soothing a complex pattern will seem because it has space to develop a rhythm. Try running your chosen pattern across an entire feature wall and then tone it down by painting the remaining walls in the pattern's dominant colour.

And finally, don't forget the power of neutrals. White, grey and shades of earth add essential breathing space to a patterned room, providing somewhere for your eye to rest. Architectural features such as skirting boards and doors are good places to go neutral, or try balancing a richly patterned scheme with some neutral furniture – a brilliant white dining table against modern, graphically patterned walls, for example, or a simple wooden coffee table in front of a statement sofa. Metal finishes such as bronze, gold and chrome have the same effect and will add an extra layer of visual interest to boot.

Design: Amelia Graham.

LIGHT & PATTERN

Light is the magical element that brings all interior schemes to life, whether plain or patterned, brightly coloured or a single shade of pale. And it is easy to get right because, unlike most other areas of decoration, lighting is more of a science than an art.

The most important thing to keep in mind is that light has a temperature, which we experience as colour. Cool light emits a white or blue tone, while warm light is yellow. Northern and morning light is cool, while southern and evening light is warm. Take a look at the room you are decorating – which direction does it face and what time of day do you use it? East-facing kitchens will be filled with the cool light of sunrise so if this is where you eat your breakfast, you might like to enhance that fresh mood with patterns based on a palette of light greens and blues. West-facing sitting rooms where you cosy up for the evening, on the other hand, are asking to be decked out in colours that reflect the warm orange glow of the setting sun. You can also use colour to change the temperature of a room: red, orange and yellow based patterns will turn up the heat in a north or east-facing room, while those featuring shades of blue, green and purple will cool things down in spaces where the light comes from the south or west.

Light temperature is measured on the Kelvin scale; the lower the number, the warmer the light. When it comes to artificial light, use the number on the bulb box as a guide. Those in the range 2000K–3000K give off a warm white/yellow glow, bulbs measuring 3100–4500K emit a cool, bright white light, while those between 4600–6500K are colder still and blueish in hue.

Light is also affected by materials. Shiny surfaces will reflect the light, while matt surfaces will absorb it, so if you want to maximize light levels, go for a feature wall of metallic wallpaper or some high-gloss floor tiles. A slubby linen sofa or a hand-woven rug, on the other hand, will create a softer, darker mood.

Ask an interior designer how to light a space and they will tell you that it's all about creating layers. Layer one is general, or ambient, light; layer two is task light used to illuminate a specific area, such as a kitchen worktop; and layer three is accent light. As the name suggests, accent light (which is generally three to five times brighter than the ambient light) is used to draw attention to certain features in a room: an artwork, architectural feature or, of course, a pattern. Accent lighting is the pattern lover's best friend – try accentuating a richly patterned sofa with a well-placed floor light, use a table lamp to highlight the pattern on a pair of curtains, or turn a collection of patterned vases into the star attraction with some LED shelf lights.

Opposite: In this grand interior, light bounces off the parquet floor, highlighting the chevron pattern and illuminating the details on the doors and shutters.

Right: Here, the shadows cast by the sunlight shining through the screen create a captivating new pattern on the floor.

ACCENT PATTERNS

Objects were made for carrying pattern. Everything that fills your home, from cushions and lampshades to vases, artworks and items of furniture, is a potential canvas for pattern, so whether you are going for full-on saturation or are just looking for a single pop to pep up a plain scheme, don't forget the stuff that lies within the walls.

Opposite: A dose of pattern can turn a piece of furniture into a work of art. Sitting this chest of drawers with its dramatic diamond print on an equally bold square-tiled floor actually reduces its visual impact because the eye has something else to focus on.

Above Left: The bold, oversized roses on the headboard give this traditional scheme a contemporary edge, while the grid-like arrangement of pictures draws attention to the subtle graphic print on the walls.

Above Right: Repeating the same pattern on a number of different decorative accessories, such as a table lamp and cushions, will lift a pared-down scheme without disturbing the overall sense of calm. Design: Identity Papers.

Above: Rather than bringing pattern to the walls with paper, try covering them with collections of objects. Here, the eclectic mix of shapes and designs is reflected in the fluid way the plates have been hung. (Arranging them in straight rows or columns would have created a more structured and orderly effect.) The simple check tablecloth brings the pattern off the wall and into the room itself, creating a sense of depth.

Opposite: Decorative objects are brilliant vehicles for pattern. This set of vases makes a bold statement against the plain and pale surroundings. Each vase is very different in pattern, colour and shape from the next, but they share a common aesthetic and geometric root so together they read as a harmonious collection.

ARCHITECTURAL FEATURES

The fabric of your house can be used as a vehicle for pattern too. Think patterned fireplaces, staircases, skirting boards, alcoves, ceilings, doors and floors.

Above: Painting the door panels in contrasting colours turns them into a feature in their own right.

Opposite (clockwise from top left): 1: A decorative grille in the partition wall has been used to add a dose of geometric pattern to an open-plan interior. **2:** Stairs were made for pattern. Here, a nature-inspired print of climbing foliage leads the eye upwards. Design: Abigail Edwards. **3:** Don't forget to look up – the ceiling is your fifth wall and it doesn't have to be plain. Design: Susi Bellamy. **4:** Tiles are a pattern-lover's best friend. Find the most vibrant you can and use them to cover a single feature. Design: Kirill Istomin.

HOW TO USE
THIS BOOK

Love Pattern & Colour sets out to seduce. Filled with images of beautiful interiors and beguiling prints, its aim is to inspire you to bring pattern into your home and make it part of your life. But it is also a practical book dedicated to equipping you with the creative knowledge and confidence you need before you embark on a decorating project.

The book is organized into eight major pattern themes: Botanicals; Geometrics; Florals; Abstracts; Cultural Travellers; Scenes & Stories; Animal Kingdom; and Textures. Introductory text provides an overview of each theme, along with some interesting nuggets of history, and then each page presents decorating possibilities to suit every style. The interior photography has been carefully chosen so that each image shows, at a glance, the impact the chosen pattern, or combination of patterns, has on the space. The accompanying captions provide detailed explanations of exactly why the scheme works and draw attention to the role key elements such as light, texture, colour and scale play in its creation.

Patterns in all their diverse forms are the book's main focus, but every one of the patterned schemes featured also has a colour palette. Colour has a profound effect on pattern. A pattern produced in red will take on an entirely different tempo from its white iteration, for example, while colour lies at the heart of successful pattern mixing.

To help explain how colour and pattern work together, we have matched many of the interior photographs with a colour bar that picks out the key palette in the scheme and provides a snapshot of the proportions of colours that make it successful.

The example on the opposite page illustrates how the colour bars work. The biggest bars are what is known as the 'ground', i.e. the two grey colours that make up three-quarters of the scheme and provide the visual anchor from which everything else springs. Notice how in this room, the grey 'ground' has been used on the furniture and accessories as well as on the wall, bringing the colour into the centre of the space. The next biggest bars are the secondary colours, which in this scheme are white and brown. The remaining part of the colour scheme comes from the accent colours – red, magenta, yellow and two different blues. These are the smallest blocks of colour on the bar, but they are also the most important; they are the pops of colour that bring the scheme to life and make this a room that you want to spend time in.

If you are immediately drawn to a particular scheme in this book then you can use the information in the accompanying caption and colour bar to help you successfully recreate it in your own interior. Alternatively, you might find that immersing yourself in Love Pattern & Colour gives you the confidence to pick and choose from lots of different schemes and create something that is entirely your own. Whichever route you take, I hope the journey is illuminating and ends in a pattern-rich home that brings you joy for years to come.

Opposite: This is a room to make you smile. It feels wonderfully playful, but it has been meticulously planned. Look closely and you will see that every pattern in room is, at heart, a celebration of the stripe. This is called the 'narrative thread' and every room should have one.

ground

accent

secondary
colour

BOTANICALS

Plants, leaves, fruits and trees have been used as decorative motifs
for millennia, from the carved stone acanthus leaves that ornament the
tops of Ancient Greek Corinthian columns, to the 'pomegranate'
pattern of Renaissance fabrics with its pine cones and thistles, and the
iron and glass beanshoots and seedpods that can still be seen decorating
the entrances to many of Paris's art nouveau Metro stations. Why have
they enjoyed such enduring popularity? The fact that the physical
structure of many plants is perfectly suited to pattern making certainly
plays a part, as does the fabulous colour palette, but essentially it
comes down to this: we are drawn to botanical images because they
remind us of the natural world and that makes us feel good.

JUNGLES & FORESTS

Combining softness with structure and spanning looks from playful, hothouse bright to lush sensuality via the stripped-back minimalism of winter trees, jungles and forests are now among the most popular sources of inspiration for contemporary pattern makers. These images show what can be achieved when you fully embrace the theme. Bold, yes, but also beautiful.

Above Left: Multi-coloured and densely patterned designs such as this need to be used over a large area and should be allowed to take centre stage. In this scheme, plain white accents give the eye a light, bright space to rest. Wood is a perfect partner for botanical themes, providing a subtle visual link back to the natural world.

Above Right: Full of fresh summer sunshine, the success of this scheme rests on the geometric motifs that run through both the wallpaper and the tiled floor. The strict blue-toned colour scheme also helps to tie the layers of pattern together. Design: Osborne & Little.

Above Left: Here, a single pattern covers both the wall and the sofa creating an immersive look. The secondary patterns on the cushions match it in both colour and scale, ensuring visual harmony. The rattan frame on the sofa continues the natural theme. Design: Nina Campbell distributed by Osborne & Little.

Above Right: This sitting room is a celebration of jungle style, but it is also a perfect example of how to combine several different bold patterns in a way that is inviting, rather than overwhelming. The primary pattern comes from the wallpaper which, with its vertical rows of trees, has a rhythm and structure that anchors the entire scheme. The more fluid lines and lighter background of the curtains and upholstery provide a balancing second layer, while the geometric patterns of the cushion and radiator cover make up the third. Design: Mindthegap.

Large-scale patterns such as these need to fill a wall, but if the wraparound foliage of the previous pages feels a step too far, then the feature wall is a good alternative. As these pictures show, restricting your vegetation to one wall in no way decreases its power to bring the space alive.

Above Left: The deep, lush green of this leaf-strewn pattern is offset by the crisp whiteness of the bed linen and side table in this feminine bedroom. The cushions provide a visual link back to the wallpaper and bring the pattern into the centre of the room, while the shot of clear blue provides a flash of contrast.

Above Right: In this contemporary-rustic scheme, the architectural elements of the room – wooden beams and the parquet floor – have been used to introduce a second layer of pattern.

Opposite: Two panels of wallpaper covered with the fronded tops of palm trees bring some welcome softness to this otherwise hard-surfaced kitchen.

The jungle and forest theme takes on a more restrained – even minimal – vibe when it is rendered in monochrome colours, or features winter trees.

Top Left: Stripped of their leaves, the straight-trunked trees covering this wallpaper give the room a pared-down, rather graphic mood, which is further enhanced by the row of pendant lights above the table.

Bottom Left: Depicted in black and white and set against the graphic lines of the white brick-tiled wall, the large, lush leaves of the jungle take on an altogether more urban look.

Opposite: The dense and vigorous jungle wallpaper brings energy and movement to this bedroom, while the striped rug adds structure and a point of visual balance. Without the paper, the scheme would fall flat; without the rug, the jungle would run riot.

Take jungle and forest patterns off the wall and onto decorative accessories. Rugs, cushions, upholstery and tableware can all be used to bring the outdoors in. Pattern-filled accessories such as these can be used either to add a bright and cheery pop to otherwise plain schemes, or as the final flourish to a maximalist look so embrace them, whatever your style, and have some fun.

Opposite: The only patterns in this sitting room are the over-scaled palm leaf on the rug and the leaf-print cushions, but the mood is pure jungle thanks to rattan furniture and a natural colour scheme.

Above Left: In this scheme, the obvious pattern element has been reduced even further. Look more closely, however, and you will see that the markings on the leaves are echoed in both the textured wall and wicker lampshade, ensuring the room is full of visual interest.

Above Right: Covering a curved sofa in a large-scale palm-tree pattern turns it into a central feature.

MEADOWS & GRASSES

Taking their inspiration from the grasses, seedheads, wild herbs and even weeds that grow in our meadows and gardens, these patterns are a prettier take on the botanical look. Less demanding than their more exotic cousins, they are easy, and joyous, to live with.

Above Left: Using the same pattern in two different colourways is an interesting, modern way to get the all-over pattern look. This is a busy design, but the simple lines of the motifs and white background mean that it doesn't overwhelm. Design: Angie Lewin for St Jude's.

Above Right: Give pretty, country-style patterns a sharper, more urban edge with a black-and-white colour palette. This monochrome take on a seedhead design would look at home in any city-chic interior.

Above Left: Cover your bed in pattern and make it the main event. In this bedroom, a large lampshade adds a second layer of pattern and, since it contains both of the key colours used, neatly ties the scheme together. A third pattern element comes from the headboard and panelling. Design: Clarissa Hulse.

Above Right: Country style meets modern luxe in this bathroom thanks to the brooding colour scheme and the juxtaposition of the delicate seedheads with strong geometric floor tiles. While the colour scheme adds drama, the seedhead design creates a soothing backdrop for a relaxing soak. Design: Little Greene.

The delicate nature of patterns inspired by meadow flowers and grasses means that you can afford to use them on a grand scale. Wrap them round the walls, run them over furniture, cover some cushions and make yourself an indoor garden.

Opposite: Small-scale pattern is very much to the fore in this sitting room, but the generous use of white keeps it feeling fresh and modern.

Above Left: In this rustic bedroom, the wallpaper, with its dancing motifs of fragile skeleton leaves, has been framed with structural beams, turning each section into a picture. The many patterns used in the room are brought together through the orange-toned colour palette.

Above Right: Strong, geometric motifs work well set against the softer, more fluid lines of botanical patterns, resulting in a scheme that is intensely patterned but comfortable to live with. Design: Nina Campbell distributed by Osborne & Little.

BOTANICAL MOTIFS

Stripped back to their essential forms, trees, leaves, fruits and all things botanical take on a graphic, modern look that suits even the most urban interiors. The shapes they create lend themselves perfectly to creating patterns, so these elementary botanical motifs provide an undeniably sophisticated edge.

Small-scale patterns such as the ones on these pages are a good way to draw attention to a specific area. The strong repeat prints bring a sense of movement, providing a path for our eye to follow.

Above Left: Pattern carries personality. This repeat of simplified trees is sunny and playful – perfect for livening up a utilitarian area of the kitchen.

Above Right: The trees on these full-length curtains have been reduced to their simplest forms. The monochrome colour scheme makes the pattern appear modern and sophisticated. Design: MissPrint.

Above Left: Sculptural and a little bit kitsch, pineapples are the pattern designer's most favourite fruit. Perfectly suited to decorative accessories, if you want to conjure tropical chic, pineapple-print cushions are the way to go. Design: Mathew Williamson at Osborne & Little.

Above Right: We all have to make room for files and paperwork in our homes, but think of the furniture that houses the unsightly stuff of life as a canvas for pattern. Decorating this nondescript bookcase with a simple outline of a tree in leaf transforms it into a painting.

Repeat prints work across larger areas too and, when the forms are soft in shape, the effect is wonderfully soothing for the soul. Whether you have a double-height wall or a compact cloakroom to work with, these bold patterns create a striking look with a comforting vibe.

Above Left: Landings and hallways are the perfect place for bold patterns as there is little in the way of furniture to compete for your attention. Here, the strong vertical lines of the trees draw the eye to the top of the stairs, encouraging you up into the rest of the house.

Above Right: One of the general rules about decorating with pattern is that the scale of the pattern should always match the scale of the room. This tiny, jewel-like cloakroom with its large-leaf wallpaper proves that rules are meant to be broken.

Opposite: The rich botanical pattern on this wallpaper is perfectly suited to the room's classical furnishings, but the slightly oversized scale and black-and-white colour scheme give it a cool, contemporary twist.

GEOMETRICS

Pinstripes and polka dots; gingham squares and fleur-de-lis; tartans and herringbones; Greek meanders and Islamic eight-point stars. Geometrics are the most versatile and ancient of pattern forms. Prehistoric peoples scratched circles and lines in the ground, the Ancient Greeks used the meander (or key) to decorate temples and objects and, thanks to their synergy with weaving, geometric designs were the first form of pattern to be used to embellish fabrics. Today, geometrics are every decorator's best friend and, in this chapter, filled with images celebrating the (almost) infinite variety and endless adaptability of geometric pattern, we show why.

STRIPES

Classic and versatile, stripes are the neutral of the pattern world. They give a room order and structure and have the power to re-shape a space. Vertical stripes draw the eye to the ceiling, making a room feel taller, while horizontal stripes elongate and create a sense of breadth.

The size of the stripe has an effect too – narrow stripes are more traditional (think of pinstripes and ticking) and will blur into a single shade when seen from a distance. Wide stripes are bolder and more contemporary. Interior design rules state that the wider the room, the broader the stripe should be, but in truth, when it comes to decorating your home, there are no rules and a wide stripe in a narrow room can be a very good look indeed.

TAILORED CHIC

Clean, sharp stripes are synonymous with all things smart and tailored. Mix with classic materials that speak of timeless sophistication such as wood, marble and leather and keep the palette simple.

Above: Broad, black-and-white stripes are always smart. Paired with sunshine yellow, they can be rather cheery too.

Opposite: In this bedroom, all the pattern is concentrated on the bed. Perfectly co-ordinated for a tailored look, the effect is softened by playful touches such as the grand canopy and the scalloped hem on the bedspread. Design: Ian Mankin.

Refined stripes can lend an air of elegance to any setting, but it's sometimes good to offset this by bringing in a touch of colourful fun. Use bright accessories or artwork for a burst of colour to really bring those oh-so-chic stripes to life.

Right: Broad, black-and-white stripes wrapped around two walls create a sense of order and rhythm in this richly furnished, formal dining room. A single yellow-striped cushion adds a pop of light-hearted colour and subtly references the yellow in the painting.

FRESH & PLAYFUL

Stripes are fun – think of beach huts, deck chairs and circus tents – so use them to inject a sense of play into your interior. The secret to creating this look is colour; blue-and-white stripes remind us of the sea, and bright colours can conjure up childhood memories. Let your imagination run wild.

Opposite: There is an essential orderliness to stripes, which means that you can disrupt them without descending into visual chaos.

Above Left: If you don't want to commit to stripes on the wall, try transforming a piece of furniture. Here, the bright vertical stripes are a witty contrast to the formal shape of the chest of drawers.

Above Right: In this sitting room, the partition has been given a bright striped makeover, the chevron design neatly reflecting the pattern on the wooden floor.

Above: This bedroom with its three layers of stripes – wood-panelled wall, cushions and sheets – is a subtle and sophisticated take on beach-hut chic.

Opposite: Fresh, nautical stripes bring energy to this simple, modern kitchen. White brick tiles provide a subtle contrast pattern and the glossy yellow fridge adds a flash of colour. End result? A room that speaks of sunshine. Design: Kirath Ghundoo.

MODERN DRAMA

Bold, wide stripes make a dramatic, contemporary statement. Try them as a single feature on a sofa, a pair of curtains or the floor, or go all out and take them over all four walls. Stripes are great mixers too, so try setting them against other patterns, or blocks of plain colour.

Opposite: A bright striped rug breaks up the block colours in this dramatic sitting room and provides a palette that links the colours of the artwork and furniture together. Design: Carpetright.

Above Left: The broad-striped upholstery on the day beds is the only printed pattern in this living space, but look closely and you will see that those straight lines are echoed in almost every surface and piece of furniture, from the yellow chair to the stark white stair treads.

Above Right: Used on a single wall, horizontal stripes make a space feel wider; wrapped around all four walls, as in this scheme, they have the opposite effect, seeming to pull the walls in, creating a cocooning effect that is welcome in this bright and airy room. Design: Studio Rhonda.

Above: Pattern carries personality. In this hallway, the bright striped stair runner instantly sets the mood for this fun, colour-filled home. The herringbone floor brings in a second layer of geometric pattern.

Opposite: This walk-in wardrobe could be an entirely functional space. Running a black-and-white striped rug along the floor injects it with a much-needed dose of energy and leads you through towards the bedroom beyond.

DOTS, SPOTS & CIRCLES

A dot is the simplest of all design elements. Anchored alone in space, it provides a focused point of attention. Of course, a single dot is not a pattern; to be a pattern, it must be joined by other dots, which can be enlarged to make spots, or hollowed out to form circles. And that's when the fun happens. Dots, spots and circles in repeat across walls, on furnishings and on objects from tableware to artwork are instantly playful, ramping up the energy in a room and raising a smile. But there is more to these motifs than fun; rounded forms are a shorthand for warmth and comfort – sensations at the heart of every home.

Opposite: Wallpaper and textiles are traditional vehicles for pattern, but if you're after a different approach, take a look at your furniture and decorative accessories. In this kitchen, richly patterned circular decals add interest to a plain wall. The spotted lampshade balances the pattern, drawing attention to the central motif.

Above Left: Plain white walls provide a calm, neutral framework for this pop-bright scheme. The wall hanging is a neat echo of the cut-outs in the sides of the occasional tables, while the straight horizontal lines of the yellow chairs inject just the right amount of contrast.

Above Right: A cluster of circular mirrors is an innovative way to introduce some pattern into an otherwise minimal space. The round shapes soften the rather austere straight lines of the staircase.

SQUARES

A square is formed when four lines, all of the same length, are joined together at right angles. These simple ingredients, always combined in the same way, create a surprisingly varied pattern group that delivers pattern and colour without visual overload. As the following images show, there's a square to suit all tastes.

Above Left: Laying squares in a random, collage-like pattern creates a more relaxed and playful effect. The square theme is reflected in the multi-coloured rug and the double glass doors.

Above Right: A bold scheme of fresh blue-and-white squares turns a staircase into a statement. The vertical and horizontal lines also give the eye a path to follow, along and up the stairs.

Opposite: Square tiles in blocks of solid colour provide the main pattern in this modern, geometric kitchen/living space, their shape subtly echoed in the cupboard, ceiling air vent and shelving. Broad horizontal stripes painted along one wall act as a counterbalance. Design: Studio Rhonda.

Opposite: Black-and-white checkerboard floor tiles are an interior classic. Here, those 'tiles' are printed onto a rug, instantly giving the look a kitsch twist. The three-dimensional cube print on the curtains carries the pattern onto the wall. Design: Jonathan Adler.

Above Left: This is a subtle, rather mid-century modern take on squares. The pattern on the wall is reflected in the veneer on the front of the console and also by the shape of the orange clock.

Above Right: The success of this chic and restful bedroom lies in the soft, grey colour scheme, which brings the various layers of pattern together. Design: Jo Hamilton Interiors.

GINGHAMS

Gingham, the simple contrasting checked fabric
synonymous with English picnics and Dorothy's dress
in *The Wizard of Oz*, is believed to have originated
in southeast Asia some 500 years ago. And it wasn't
a check at all, but a stripe. (The name comes from the
Malayan word *genggang*, meaning 'striped'.) However,
when the fabric came to England in the late seventeenth
century, the Manchester mills began to weave it into

a checked pattern and a classic was born. Endlessly
versatile, gingham can be used on everything from
furnishings to tableware and in every style of interior –
all it takes is a change of scale and colourway. Small
checks in shades of pale create a pattern so subtle that
it simply adds depth to a room, but opt for something big
and bold, such as a citrus bright or black and white, and
it takes centre stage.

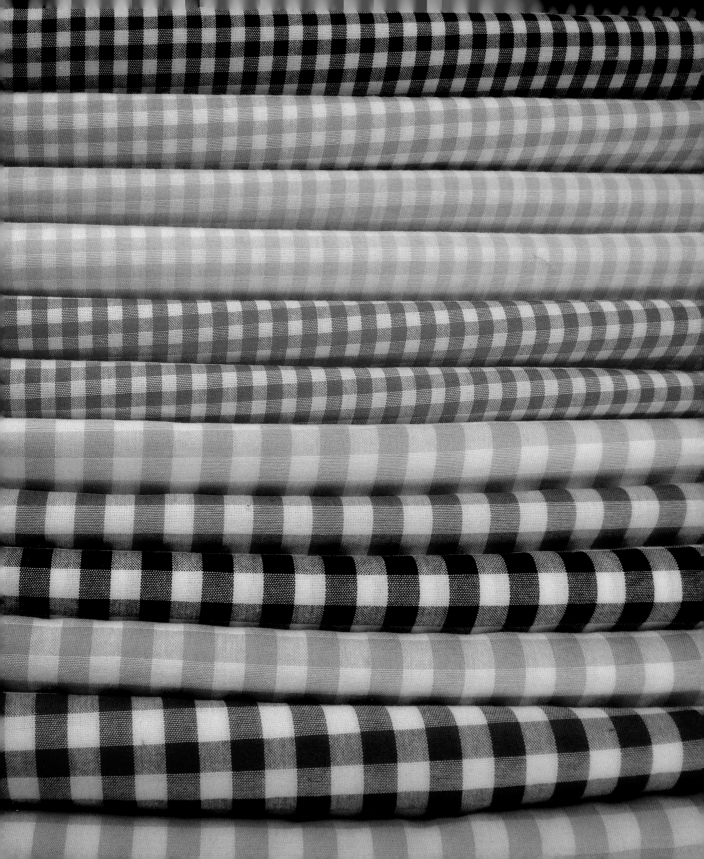

HOUNDSTOOTH

Houndstooth, so called because it looks like dogs' teeth, is made up of small, broken, slanting checks. Always two-tone, it is most often seen in black and white. It originated in Scotland in the 1800s as a woven wool cloth worn by shepherds, and soon became a fashion classic. With all the elegance of tweed but a dash more dynamism, houndstooth made the transition into interiors in the twentieth century where it has enjoyed lasting popularity.

Opposite: Used to cover both the hallway floor and the stairs, houndstooth adds drama, energy and depth to what is often a rather featureless area of the house. The movement in the pattern acts as an invitation to come in and up the stairs. The small scale of the pattern also means it won't show the dirt, which is a useful characteristic in a heavy-traffic area. Design: Carpetright.

Above: Small-scale patterns in tight repeats such as houndstooth read more as texture than pattern, making them a good way to create a focal point in an otherwise plain scheme.

Left: Large tweed cushions bring some textural pattern to a classic leather chesterfield in this sitting room. The subtle geometric pattern of the cloth is reflected in, and emphasized by, the exposed brick wall and wooden floor. Design: Barker & Stonehouse.

Opposite: A single cushion made from a modern, multi-coloured take on tweed fills this space with warmth, texture and energy.

TARTANS & TWEEDS

The origin of tartan is the subject of much debate (ancient samples of chequered cloths have been found right across Europe and Scandinavia), but whatever its past, the pattern has become synonymous with Scotland. Tweed too has its roots in the country, where it started life as a logical response to the elements. Highland weather is harsh and sheep are plentiful so, naturally, people wove their wool into hard-wearing clothes. In the nineteenth century, high-quality weaving made these fabrics popular outside their traditional home and they became shorthand for British tradition and smart country lifestyle. If you wanted to look like a landowner, you dressed yourself in tartan and tweed. However, as fashion designers from Vivienne Westwood to Alexander McQueen have shown, there is an altogether edgier side to these fabrics; it's just a question of how you use them. And as these images show, the same is true for interiors, so whether your taste is for trad and timeless or cool and modern, take a look at tartan and tweed.

Take my will and my life.
Guide me in my recovery.
Show me how to live.

Opposite: Tartan gets an urban update in this study. The square picture frames draw further attention to the checked walls, while the striped lampshade provides a note of contrast.

Above Left: Floors were made for pattern. This slightly abstracted take on tartan fills a contemporary living space with life and warmth and colour.

Above Right: A mix of warm-coloured tartans set against a wood-panelled wall creates a modern hunting-lodge vibe. The long, horizontal stripes of both the wall and floor provide a nice note of contrast, framing the check details inside the room itself.

OTHER GEOMETRIC MOTIFS

Hexagons, triangles, stars, diamonds, rectangles, zigzags, spirals... the list of geometric shapes is long and each one is perfectly suited for pattern making. The images on these pages offer a taste of what wondrous patterns can be formed when a number of curves, points and lines are joined together.

Top Left: Diamonds are a fun motif for a child's bedroom and the clean lines create a welcome sense of order. Changing the colour and direction of the repeat is a good way to add layers of interest without overloading the space with pattern.

Bottom Left: In this home office, a triangle repeat acts as a visual link between the organic forms of the wallpaper and the strict geometry of the desk.

Opposite: A chest of drawers painted in a striking black-and-white diamond pattern takes centre stage in this hallway. The sense of geometry is enhanced by the wallpaper, which at first glance looks like a floral, but is in fact another diamond.

Opposite: In this pattern, curving ribbons are arranged in straight horizontal lines resulting in a design that has both energy and a rhythm soothing enough to live with. Design: MissPrint.

Top Right: Because there are no gaps between the shapes, tessellating patterns can be too dominant in a room. Here, only the outline of the motif is coloured, leaving lots of quiet, white space. The tightness of the repeat also means that the individual motifs appear to merge, creating a sense more of texture than pattern.

Bottom Right: Abstracted triangles resembling mountain peaks dance across this wallpaper, their sharp points softened by those sun-bright yellow circles. Design: MissPrint.

Left: There are three main layers of pattern in this mid-century modern kitchen: the rectangular, brick-like tiles on the wall; the horizontal wood veining on the cabinets; and the woven zigzag lines of the rug. Each is quite distinct but they are united by their shared linear structure.

Opposite: This scheme takes geometric mixing to the maximum and, while it may not be everyone's idea of a liveable living space, it does demonstrate how the formal structure of geometric shapes allows you to pile pattern on top of pattern without descending into visual chaos. The dominant pattern is the stripe on the rug, which is reflected in the secondary layer on the wall. The repeat on this paper is so tight, the busy pattern recedes into texture when viewed from a distance. The third layer is provided by the furniture and decorative accessories – the chest of drawers, stool, cushions and mirror – where, again, straight lines impose a sense of order. A few well-placed curves bring a hint of softness to the scheme.
Design: Jonathan Adler.

MIX IT UP

Mixing patterns adds another layer of complexity to an interior scheme, which creates intricacy and, since our brains are stimulated by intricacy, we tend to find combinations of patterns aesthetically appealing. Maximalism is also back in fashion, which means there has never been a better time to embrace the multi-pattern look. And, since the secret of successful mixing lies in finding a common theme to link all the patterns together, geometrics, with their shared mathematical foundation, are made to go together.

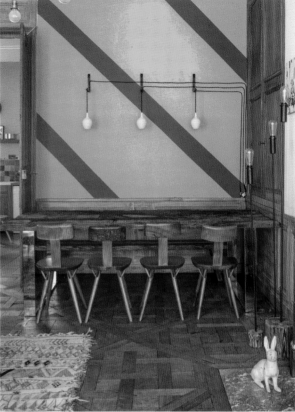

Opposite: Complex pattern combinations such as these need space. Running the two main patterns across the wall and the floor allows them room to develop a rhythm that reduces the tempo. The strict black-and-white colour scheme ties each of the six patterns together.

Above Left: A riot of geometric motifs come together in this contemporary living space. White walls and bold blocks of solid colour create welcome pauses between the patterns. The simple shapes of the furniture and artworks echo the geometric theme, which also helps to create a sense of visual cohesion.

Above Right: This dining room demonstrates that multi-patterned living has a quieter side too. The broad diagonal lines painted across the back wall make a bold, graphic statement that is subtly echoed in, and balanced by, the herringbone pattern of the wooden floor and the simple geometric motifs in the rug.

FLORALS

'Flowers are happy things', said the English author and humourist PG Wodehouse. He wasn't, as far as we know, attempting to explain the perennial appeal of floral patterns in interior design, but he could have been. Like their cousins the botanicals, flowers have been inspiring designers for as long as there have been furniture, textile, wallpaper and surface designers seeking inspiration and, while their exhilarating variety of scales, colours and shapes is certainly a factor, the real allure of flowers lies in their ability to lift the spirits of everyone who sees them. The following pages celebrate contemporary flower power in all its beautiful variety. Read on and feel the joy bloom.

Left: The painters of the Dutch Golden Age knew all about using dark colours to bring out the drama of hothouse flowers. In this Gothic-meets-country-cottage bedroom, an opulent floral wall meets a herringbone-patterned parquet floor; the roundness of the flower heads is offset by the sharp angles of the wooden blocks.

Opposite: Pastel colours and clouds of garden roses give this floral pattern a chintz-like feel that, on a smaller scale, would be too traditional for the simple, contemporary furniture in this bedroom. Blown up to giant size, however, the pattern instantly transforms into something bold and super modern. Pretty, pastel colours and a painterly approach keep the room feeling soft, while the graphic leaf print on the throw injects a note of geometric structure. Design: Wallsauce.

FLORAL EXPLOSION

Fashions for floral patterns have come and gone. In the mid-eighteenth century, small sprigs of flowers became hugely popular decorative motifs in Europe thanks to the invention of wallpaper-printing machines. Up until this point, wallpapers had been painted or blocked by hand, making them the preserve of the rich; mass production sent prices tumbling, allowing the mass population to bring pattern onto their interior walls too. These patterns were small and floral because they were the easiest motifs to print, but as machinery became more sophisticated, the flowers grew ever larger and brighter, finally bursting into the riot of hyperreal blooms that characterized the Victorian era.

By the turn of the century, a quieter, more stylized take on floral patterns started to emerge. In the UK, textile designer William Morris turned his back on the march of machine production, reviving hand-made processes such as block printing and traditional weaving. Going back to basics meant embracing simpler forms of pattern too, with flatter floral motifs that suggested, rather than imitated, the blooms that inspired them. Elsewhere in the world, art nouveau took a similar approach, depicting flowers as geometric forms.

Modernism and its disdain for ornamentation in a world where form followed function led to a decline in the popularity of floral patterns in the twentieth century. There were brief revivals: pretty, sprigged florals made a comeback for curtains and upholstery in the 1950s; the 1970s saw both a return to busy flower patterns and a new craze for large-scale florals in saturated, psychedelic colours; while the 1980s were all about the country cottage garden. The twenty-first century, however, has been good for fans of all things floral and today, when it comes to this look, more is most definitely more!

Above Left: Flower patterns bloom from every surface and on every object in this scheme. It is certainly busy, but the layers of pattern are so perfectly combined that the overall effect is rather harmonious and soothing. The bright yellow design on the bed is the dominant pattern, anchored by the tight, almost textural, repeat on the back wall. The upholstered furniture and lampshades introduce pops of accent pattern, all linked by motif and colour. The symmetrical layout provides a highly structured framework that gives the scheme a satisfying sense of order. Design: Mindthegap.

Above Right: This is all opulent glamour thanks to the luxurious materials (velvet upholstery, silk curtains, polished wood floor) and rich colour scheme. There is only one pattern here, but the different colourways mean that each one stands alone, adding to the sumptuous atmosphere.

Opposite: In these two schemes, the same floral print has been used on both the furniture and the walls, creating spaces filled with the sweet nostalgia of a country garden in summertime. In both rooms, plenty of plain white space provides just the right note of modernity.

These images show the kitsch face of full-on florals. Whether you like retro styles or Mexican-inspired designs in the brightest of contrasting colours, florals can help create smile-raising schemes in your home.

Above Right: Decorated in a pastel version of the same pattern, this attic bedroom would have been pure country cottage, but in electric blue and sugar-mouse pink, it takes on an altogether funkier feel. Plain white bedding and a geometric-print cushion add a clean, modern note.

Opposite: Exotic blooms in the hot, saturated colours of the tropics take centre stage in this cheerful dining room. Light-hearted it may be, but the patterns on the tablecloth and rug have been carefully chosen to complement each other both in colour (they share the same shade of orange) and scale (the flowers on the rug are smaller than those on the cloth), ensuring the scheme makes visual sense.

Above Left: Here, a cute flowerpot repeat has been used to bring some retro fun to a kitchen wall. The variation in the scale of the motif as it crosses the wall creates a slightly three-dimensional effect, which would bring a sense of depth to a small room.

If you want a floral explosion without total immersion, then embrace the power of the plain wall. A bold, colourful print can take centre stage when placed against a plain backdrop, helping the pattern unleash its full potential as the focus of the room.

Opposite: If light walls lift and freshen, dark walls bring elegance and drama. Here, the deep grey/blue panelled wall provides a sophisticated, contemporary backdrop for the rather traditional floral pattern on the sofa and curtains. The blocks of solid colour also act as a breathing space between the patterns, allowing each to stand alone and therefore increasing, rather than diminishing, their impact.
Design: Osborne & Little.

Above: In this scheme, an elegant, high-backed sofa covered in a super bright flower print sits in front of a plain, pale wall which allows the bold pattern to sing out. Using wall-mounted floral plates to bring in another layer of pattern is very effective – the undulating arrangement and different sizes of both plate and pattern introduce a sense of movement.

ABSTRACTED FLORALS

Reduced to their simplest forms, flowers become graphic motifs; assemblages of shapes that can be used in repeat to create patterns that bridge the divide between loose and formal, pretty and urban, traditional and modern. Popular with pattern makers such as British textile designer Lucienne Day and Finnish brand Marimekko during the height of Modernism, and revived in recent years by pattern queen Orla Kiely, this is a pared-back take on flowers. If you think florals are not for you, take a look at the patterns on the following pages and think again.

Above: Blue pops against mustard yellow in this pairing, while a common sense of geometry, shared floral theme and flashes of white ensure visual harmony between the two prints. Right: Design: MissPrint.

Opposite: This is an unusual combination and, at first glance, the two patterns seem to have little in common. However, both motifs share the same jagged, slightly cartoonish, profile and the black centre of each poppy finds its echo in the bunch of grapes on the opposite print. Left: Design: Marimekko. Right: Design: Neisha Crosland.

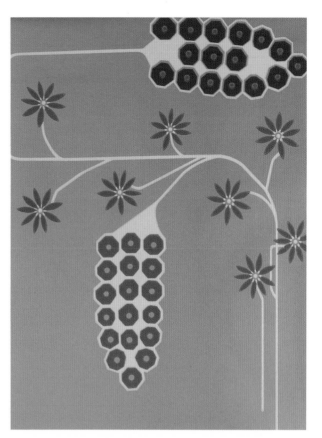

The simplicity and structure of abstracted florals means they are perfectly suited for large-scale use – in fact, just as with geometrics, you will find that the more space you give these patterns, the less attention they demand because they have room to take on a soothing rhythm.

Opposite: This is an unashamedly sweet and pretty print, but the slightly abstracted form of the floral sprigs injects just the right note of modern sophistication. Design: MissPrint.

Above Left: In this multi-layered floral scheme, the largest pattern is on the day bed, which makes it the focal point, cleverly drawing our attention away from the busy decoration and towards the function of the space. The cheerful sunflower repeat on the wall provides a balancing second layer of pattern, while the cushions and stool act as that all-important third element. The cut velvet fabric on the stool introduces an interesting textural note too.

Above Right: There is a lot of pattern in this sitting room – it covers the wall, full-length curtains and the mass of cushions on the sofa – but the overall effect is rather calm, minimal even. This is partly due to the pale colour scheme of course, but the patterns themselves are crucial to the effect. The large-scale flower repeat on the back wall is so reduced as to be more geometric than floral, while the tightness of the repeat on the curtains means they recede slightly, becoming an almost textural element in the scheme. The cushions reflect the central, graphic floral theme and bring the look together.

Used in a small area, abstracted floral patterns are transformed into little works of art, drawing the eye or creating a harmonious link between the other elements of the room.

Above: A beautiful embroidered bedspread takes pride of place here, its central, rather angular, floral motif echoed on the large turquoise cushion. This is a sumptuous look, full of the flavours of Morocco – proof that abstracted florals can be just as extravagant as their more naturalistic cousins.

Opposite: The floor becomes the focal point in this sitting room thanks to the rug with its rows of oversized, super-simplified sunflowers. A striped fire surround subtly reflects the linear arrangement of the motif, while the abstracted pear print on the cushion mirrors the simplicity and scale of the sunflower.

Opposite: There are five different floral prints in this bedroom. It works because the three dominant prints – the chair, the wallpaper and the duvet cover – all balance each other out in terms of scale, while the quilt and the cushion provide smaller, secondary layers. The striped pillow adds a note of quiet geometry and reflects the major colours in the room.
Design: fabric: Abigail Borg; upholstery: Florrie+Bill.

Right: With its unusual colour scheme and large-scale motif, this is classic country garden made modern.
Design: Abigail Borg.

COUNTRY GARDEN

Floral patterns have often focused on exotic flowers from far-flung countries, a trend that began with the expansion of global trade and travel and continues to this day because these mysterious and unfamiliar blooms imbue our surroundings with a sense of adventure and sophistication. However, there is also a counter floral trend, which focuses on what can be found growing outside our own front doors. Proudly pretty and wonderfully familiar, these country garden patterns may not make us feel as though we are on holiday, but they do make us feel at home.

Full of colour and printed with such tight repeats they barely seem to be there at all, the papers in these images turn the walls they cover into glorious fields of flowers.

Top Left: Unashamedly pretty, this scheme embraces the nostalgia of spriggy floral patterns. Using the carved frames of the mirror and sconces to bring in a second layer of pattern allows the flowers to stand out, while also adding depth and interest to the scheme.

Bottom Left: This is a perfect example of the power of a feature wall. Used on a larger scale, this bright floral pattern would have receded slightly as the repeat became noticeable. Restricted to a single wall, however, it pops like a giant painting, filling the room with cheerful energy.

Opposite: With its oversized agapanthus heads and ordered repeat, this wallpaper shows the more modern, urban face of the country garden. In this room it has been used on its own, but this is a pattern made for layering thanks to the graphic simplicity of the motif. Emphasize the contemporary by going for a couple of abstracted florals (remember, when it comes to mixing patterns, odd numbers are best), or introduce a more rural note with something small and spriggy like the patterns to the left. Design: Tracy Kendall.

For a less full-on take on the country look, leave the walls plain and run your patterns over decorative accessories from cushions and tableware to rugs, lampshades and bedheads.

Opposite: The essence of country-cottage chic, this sitting room relies solely on the power of the patterned textiles. The small, trailing floral motifs are balanced by the geometry of the patchwork on the crocheted throw.

Above: If you are going all-out for the country-garden look then dressing a table in a riot of floral patterns will be a final flourish. Alternatively, if you're not sure this is the aesthetic for you, it's a really good way to experiment. Table settings are temporary so you can afford to be over the top; forget the pattern-mixing guidelines and let yourself go.

Above: Co-ordination has rather gone out of fashion, but as this matching headboard and lampshade combination proves, done right, it can be a very good look indeed. The pattern is wonderfully old fashioned, conjuring images of rambling cottage gardens, but the deep-blue ground gives it a sophisticated, modern feel. Design: Abigail Borg.

Opposite: The cushions in this image all have different patterns, but they share a floral theme and colour palette. The broad stripe of the sofa seat provides a nice graphic contrast, while the blurred edges of each stripe echo the rustic garden feel.

Above Left: Turn an old cabinet into a feature filled with the spirit of the country. Here, some swatches of flower-patterned fabric have replaced the glass in the top cupboard, with the pretty trailing patterns and pastel colours reflected in the crockery below.

Above Right: Adding a trailing rose to the front of the cupboard instantly injects personality and movement into this rather plain home office.

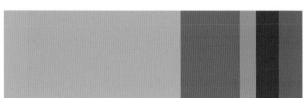

Above Left: Here, a featureless modern sideboard has been turned into a floral art piece. The more open, large-scale pattern on the wallpaper panel is a balancing contrast to the busyness of the primary pattern.

Above Right: In this scheme, a sofa upholstered in a trailing, country-garden pattern sits in front of a flat, abstracted floral repeat. The result is rich and cocooning, the pattern on the wall bringing a sense of depth to the room and grounding the lighter, prettier pattern of the fabric. Design: Mindthegap.

ABSTRACTS

In abstract patterns, the visual language of shape, form, line and colour
is used to create a decorative composition that contains no recognizable
objects, scenes or figures. The beauty of these impressionistic designs is
that they are great mixers, happily coexisting with, and even enhancing,
other patterns in the room.

ABSTRACT MOTIFS

Even abstracted patterns begin with a motif. In these images, that motif is still just recognizable – the loose swirls on the walls of the dusty pink dining room form into a rose if you look long enough, and the sinuous shapes painted on the wooden boards of the hallway have their roots in the teardrop forms of paisley. Bridging the gap between realism and absolute abstraction, patterns such as these are bold and contemporary but also surprisingly versatile, particularly if you opt for a muted colour palette.

Above: Simplifying the motif until it is the merest suggestion of a rose means that the supersized scale of the pattern doesn't overpower this dining room. The smaller, busier, abstracted design on the rug creates a sense of balance.

Opposite: A bold, curling floor pattern brings drama and energy to this otherwise plain space. (If you're unsure about using bold patterns, then the floor is a great place to experiment because, unlike a wall, you don't look at it head-on.)

If your taste runs towards the geometric but you're after something a little less ordered, then abstracted versions of classic geometric forms are a good option. Patterns such as these need space to develop a soothing rhythm (confine them and they become over-busy), so use them on walls or floors rather than furniture and accessories.

Opposite: Horizontal lines make a room feel wider, but they can be too bold a statement. This abstracted version, in which the lines gently undulate across the wall, creates the same space-enhancing effect in an altogether softer way. Design: MissPrint.

Above Left: In this bathroom, small mosaic tiles have been arranged in a complex web of irregular diamond shapes. The pixelated nature of the mosaic echoes the veins in the marble floor, bringing a welcome sense of texture to what could be a rather cold scheme. The plain wall creates a breathing space, while the reflection in the mirror adds an extra layer, giving a feeling of depth.

Above Right: Here, an elaborate Rococo-esque motif has been pared back until it is only just recognizable. The distinctive, ordered repeat – unusual for an abstract pattern – is softened by the ombre finish. The gradual change in tone also draws the eye upwards, making the room appear taller. Design: Identity Papers.

Swirling forms in such tight repeats that there appears to be no repeat at all are full of drama and energy. Give them space and use them in areas where they can take centre stage, such as a bedroom or hallway, and the effect is surprisingly restful.

Above: Incidental, transitional spaces such as landings and hallways are perfect places to try out bold patterns. Here, the scribble-like pattern draws the eye along the entrance hall, encouraging you in. The movement in the pattern makes this otherwise plain white corridor pop. Design: interior: Kate Watson-Smyth of madaboutthehouse.com; runner: Ella Doran for Alternative Flooring.

Opposite: The only other pattern in this bedroom is a single gold stripe on the bed linen, which reflects the gold in the paper and also acts as a balance for the curved forms swirling above. Running the pattern over the ceiling turns the room into a luxurious and cocooning boudoir. Design: Graham & Brown x Barbara Hulanicki.

MARBLING

Marble is a byword for classical grandeur; it is the material of the Taj Mahal and the Colosseum, Venus de Milo and Michelangelo's David. It is also a rich and wonderful carrier of pattern, thanks to those natural veins and colour gradations. The pattern-shy can use it to introduce a dash of texture and visual interest to an otherwise plain interior, while for pattern lovers, its subtlety means it almost reads as a plain and can therefore provide that all-important breathing space in an otherwise pattern-rich scheme. And you don't even

have to go for the real thing. Thanks to marble's recent return to high fashion, designers across the world are producing wallpapers and furnishing fabrics that have all the visual appeal of the actual stone but without the high prices and tricky installation process.

Marble is most commonly found in bathrooms, hallways and kitchens, but the rise of marble-effect wallpaper means you can bring it into other less traditional spaces too.

Opposite Left: Nothing says luxe living quite like a wraparound marble room. Here, the natural, random patterning in the stone has been anchored by the ordered repeat pattern of the cornice.

Opposite Right: A dramatic marble-effect feature wall marks out the dining area of this contemporary open-plan space. The strong geometric lines that run through the more organic veining keep the pattern clear and simple, maintaining the clean lines of this otherwise plain interior. Design: wall covering: Fromental; designer: Maddux Creative.

Above Left: This soft, almost textured, marble-like wallpaper is a perfect backdrop for the bold pattern of the sofa, reflecting the colours and adding a sense of depth.
Design: Designers Guild.

Above Right: The marble pattern takes centre stage in this bedroom. Rather than introduce additional printed patterns, which would be overwhelming in a room meant for sleeping, the strong feature wall is balanced by points of textural pattern in the throw on the bed and buttoned bench at its foot.

Marble isn't only for walls and floors. Its mottled colours and intricate lines can be found ornamenting and beautifying all manner of things, from furniture to fabric and fireplaces.

Above: A marble-topped console has been used to add a second layer of pattern in this hallway. The grey tones pick out the pale branches of the floral wallpaper, tying the scheme together.

Opposite: Even minimal interiors can incorporate a dash of marble. In this white-walled room, a richly veined marble fire surround has been used to add both pattern and texture, without compromising the simplicity of the scheme.

PAINTERLY

The ultimate in abstraction, the patterns on these pages take their inspiration from the art world. Think fluid shapes, visible brush strokes, soft sweeps of watercolour and great dollops of paint, splattered and left to run. Freely formed and without any obvious repeat, painterly patterns are amongst the easiest to live with, providing a backdrop for other patterns, furniture and the stuff of day-to-day life. Unless you choose to go bold, of course...

These images show what can be done when you embrace the quieter side of painterly patterns. In each scheme, the subtle gradations of colour and evident brush markings bring a sense of texture as well as visible pattern to the spaces, which have otherwise been left pattern-free. As you can see from the photographs, this is a versatile look, as effective in small spaces as it is over large areas.

Above: Broad sweeps of colour provide the pattern element in both these schemes. In the sitting room (left), a teal arc sits against a stripe of brooding, chalky grey. The mottled rug and soft folds of fabric falling through the diamond-shaped holes of the chair frame provide secondary notes of pattern and texture. The dining booth (right) is more subtle still, appearing plain until you get close enough to see the curved lines striping across the walls. Right: Design: Jill Malek.

Opposite: The paint effect on the wall of this classically elegant living room is so textural that it could be fabric and the effect is to imbue the space with a welcoming sense of warmth that doesn't detract from its chic simplicity. The straight lines running through the pattern draw the eye to the wooden panelling on the adjoining wall. Design: Jill Malek.

CULTURAL
TRAVELLERS

———

Pattern making is a universal instinct and every country in the world has its own traditions and techniques. The following pages contain a taste of some of the patterns – from the ikats of Indonesia to paisley and the mesmerizing complexity of Islamic arabesques – that have crossed countries and continents, casting their influence on aesthetics far from home.

IKAT

Ikat is a dyeing technique in which the surface design is created in the yarns themselves, rather than on the finished cloth. Characterized by its vibrant, slightly blurred, colours and double-sided pattern, there is evidence of ikat making in pre-Columbian Peru and tenth-century Yemen, as well as Japan, India and Uzbekistan, but it is generally believed to have originated in Indonesia. (The name comes from the Malay-Indonesian word 'mengikat', meaning to tie or to bind.) The fabric arrived in Europe via Dutch, Spanish and Portuguese traders in Southeast Asia, and from merchants who stopped at the Uzbek ikat centres of Samarkand and Bukhara as they made their way along the Silk Road.

Like tie-dye, ikat is made using a 'resist' process in which individual yarns, or bundles of yarn, are bound together in the pattern the maker desires and then dyed. The binding is made from a dye-resistant material (plastic thread or rubber bands are commonly used today) so that the yarns beneath it remain colour-free. The process is often repeated many times with different dyes and binding arrangements to create multi-coloured patterns. When the maker is satisfied, the yarns are released from their bindings and woven into cloth. Creating the pattern in the yarns themselves, rather than through the weaving or printing processes, means that ikat fabrics are patterned on both sides.

Another distinguishing feature of ikat textiles is the slight blurring of the pattern edges. This appealing characteristic is actually a result of weaver error – lining up all the dyed yarns so that the pattern comes out perfectly clean on the finished cloth is extremely difficult, and the slightest misalignment results in a blur – but there is beauty in imperfection and blurriness is much prized by the fabric's many fans.

Painterly, timeless and imbued with a sense of craftsmanship, it's no wonder ikat has travelled the world.

The graphic simplicity of ikat designs means that they are made for mixing. Geometric patterns are their ideal partner, so embrace all things striped, checked, spotted and spiralled and discover the spirit-lifting power of compound pattern.

Opposite: Using the same pattern across different applications creates an immersive look that is both bold and rather cocooning. Introducing an alternative colourway and a pop of complimentary pattern stops this pairing merging into one. Design: Manuel Canovas at Colefax and Fowler.

Above Left: Here, changes in the weight of the primary pattern – solid motifs mixed with outlines – bring energy to the space and stop it feeling overly co-ordinated and flat.

Above Right: Plenty of plain white space and a multi-coloured table runner are the magic ingredients in this scheme. The striped cloth pulls all the various colours together, while the white spaces give each pattern room to breathe.

Above: Classic meets modern in this sitting room thanks to the pattern clash of chair and rug. The pairing breaks all the guidelines – the scales are the same, while the colours are not – but somehow it works, proving that, when it comes to interior design, the most important things are beautiful raw ingredients and plenty of confidence.

Opposite: An outsized ikat rug turns the floor into a striking focal point in this sitting room. It is balanced by a pair of matching armchairs, upholstered in a small-scale repeat that neatly reflects the jagged edge of the diamonds. Furniture can get lost on a boldly patterned floor; here, strong colours make sure the chairs and stools stand out.

AFRICAN INSPIRATION

Africa offers an entire continent of patterns, from the simple, graphic motifs of Malian mud cloth (or 'bogolanfini') in the West to the red-check Shuka cloth worn by the Maasai people of East Africa. Found ornamenting architecture, objects, artefacts, jewellery, textiles and the human body, these patterns are often rich in meaning, acting as markers of social and cultural identity. The circles and lines, dots and dashes painted on the mud cloths of Mali, for example, tell of family histories; the stories and their symbols are passed down from mother to daughter.

However, while there is no such thing as a universal 'African pattern', geometric shapes, particularly chevrons, zigzags, diamonds and triangles, exist in almost every form of African decoration. Drawing on a colour palette inspired by nature and arranged in both organized repeats and more random scatterings, these are timeless patterns you will want to live with.

Opposite: This intricate tribal design wallpaper features a traditional cloth pattern called called 'Ashoke'. These cloths are hand-woven and worn by the Yoruba people of Nigeria, usually at major ceremonies.
Design: Mindthegap.

Right: These prints are certainly bold, but the simplicity of the lines and restricted colour palette make them surprisingly easy to incorporate into almost any style of interior. Top: Design: Amelia Graham for Sunbury Design. Bottom: Design: Mindthegap.

Right: This contemporary, light-feeling living room is surprisingly full of pattern. The three richly patterned cushions, inspired by African textiles, are the star attraction, but the room's calm, harmonious spirit is a result of the framework provided by the textural pattern on the floor, and that pale horizontal stripe of the curtains around two of the four walls. Design: Amelia Graham/Studio 2LG.

Embrace the vibrant colourscape of the African continent with patterned accessories from table lamps to tableware. Objects are a great way to introduce pops of pattern into a scheme and also allow you to test whether you enjoy living with a particular style before investing in wallpapers or furnishing fabrics.

Top Left: Travel souvenirs such as this nest of woven bowls are a quick and easy way to inject a pop of authentic colour and pattern into your home.

Bottom Left: If you are going to mix lots of patterns then you need to find a unifying theme. Here, six different patterns are brought together with woven texture. Restricting the patterns to a single type of object also brings visual harmony.
Design: RE (RE-foundobjects).

Opposite: Used on their own, bold patterns become statement-making works of art. In this study, the wall hanging is balanced by the subtly patterned surfaces of the woven lampshade and stool cover.

Clean, geometric prints and a monochrome colour scheme allow you to create an interior that conjures the spirit of African design without falling into pastiche.

Opposite: The secret to using lots of different patterns in a small space is to restrict your colours and style of motif. In this scheme, everything is black or white and the patterns share a geometric root. Rather than varying the scale, as is usual with combinations of pattern, here they are all on the small side, which creates a rather textural effect that lowers the tempo of the room. Design: Debenhams.

Above: In this monochrome dining room, the table runner takes centre stage, its strong, linear pattern echoed in the wooden screen across the back wall and subtly reflected in the shape of the stool in the foreground.

Left: Embroidery has a long tradition in Mexico. This fabric, with its exquisitely sewn flowers and hothouse colours, would bring a sense of energy, fun and authentic craftsmanship to any interior.

Opposite: This outdoor sitting room is a riot of vibrant colour and diverse pattern, but at its heart are the two sarape blankets wrapped over the seat of the sofa. The simple, broad stripes act as a visual anchor and provide a palette of colours for the rest of the scheme.

INSPIRED BY MEXICO

Mexican patterns are synonymous with sharp geometry, embroidered animals and the broad stripes of sarape blankets. Many of these patterns have their roots in the Aztec Empire and the textile art of its people, the Nahuas. With no formal written language, the Nahuas developed an intricate system of symbols that were used to ornament everything from clothing to buildings and artwork. These symbols were a method of communication, telling of identity, social status and religion, but rendered in vivid colours – pink, turquoise blue, and yellow the hue of gleaming gold bars – they were also extremely decorative, which is why they hold such appeal for us today. These ancient patterns pack a punch, turn up the heat and bring joy to the spaces they inhabit.

Filling a room with Mexican-inspired pattern certainly turns up the energy dial, but it doesn't have to be exhausting to live with. The secret is to add plenty of natural materials and finish with a sprinkling of calmer, contrasting prints.

Opposite: Eclectic pattern clashes will always raise the heart rate, but by keeping the motifs on theme (floral) and the colour palette tight (shades of red to pink), this scheme avoids tipping into visual overload.

Top Right: The artworks carry most of the pattern and colour in this dining room and, since each piece is framed by an area of clean, white space, there are plenty of visual resting places to quieten the mood. The visible grain on the floor tiles adds a layer of textural pattern, which fills the room with a sense of depth and warmth.

Bottom Right: More amounts to less in this bedroom. The hot pattern on the bedspread makes the room pop, but the stripes of the wood-panelled wall and the abstract geometry of the Aztec-style rug create a layered effect that calms the space down.

Bring the patterns and colours of Mexico into your home with a feature rug, beautifully patterned chair or perfectly curated collection of objects.

Above Left: This apparently simple scheme contains three layers of geometric pattern – the vivid stripes of the blankets, the tight mesh of the chair and the large checkerboard tiles on the floor. The dancing line of painted figures on the wall adds a welcome sense of movement.

Above Right: Hallways are wonderful canvases for experimentation and a little bit of theatre. Here, an ornate coatrack and collection of brightly patterned bags turn a utilitarian, often neglected, space into a patterned tableau. And since the bags can be used to contain everyday clutter like dog leads and gloves, it's satisfyingly functional too.

Opposite: This contemporary living room is full of the spirit of Mexico. Aztec-inspired patterns on the twin chairs and rug raise the tempo, while blocks of plain colour create plenty of space for the eye to rest. Design: Suzy Hoodless.

PAISLEY

This iconic motif gets its English name from the Scottish town of Paisley, but its origins lie in Persia where the familiar droplet, known as the 'boteh', is believed to have represented a cluster of leaves, shrub or flower bud.

It was Kashmir shawls, brought along the silk routes by the East India Company in the eighteenth century, which first introduced the pattern to Europe. The original shawls were priced beyond the reach of all but the super rich, so enterprising manufacturers – particularly in Paisley – soon started making their own. A craze was born.

A favourite of key art and design styles from the Arts and Crafts and Aesthetic movements to art nouveau, paisley became an emblem of all things bohemian, its Eastern symbolism making it The Beatles' pattern of choice in the 1960s. John Lennon even put it on his car.

Over half a century later, paisley patterns are still in fashion, particularly for interiors where that distinctive swirling motif proves surprisingly adaptable.

171

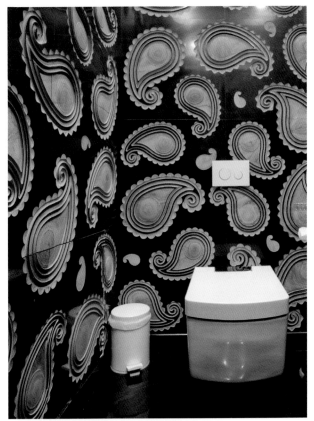

Opposite: This elegant scheme marries a swirling, large-scale paisley with strong geometric patterns for a modern take on tradition. Muted colours tone down the impact of the pattern.

Above Left: Supersizing the iconic paisley motif instantly ups the impact of the pattern. Bold patterns like this are perfect for cloakrooms where they don't have to compete with furniture and, since no one stays long, you can afford to have some fun.

Above Right: Paisley and gingham come together in this bedroom. The black-and-white colour scheme, punctuated with a pop of brilliant red, gives patterns often associated with country style a sharper, more urban feel.

These images showing two colourways of the same paisley print demonstrate the versatility of this age-old pattern. In both rooms, the busy pattern is offset by plenty of plain, solid colour which allows it to stand out but not overwhelm.

Above: In navy and sand, paisley becomes sophisticated enough for a city centre apartment. Design: Zara Home.

Opposite: In pink, paisley is the essence of country cottage prettiness. Design: Zara Home.

ISLAMIC INFLUENCES

Islamic decoration can be broadly divided into three forms: geometric patterns, calligraphy and the arabesque, which is based on the curved and branching forms of plants and is the floral style of Islamic design. Stemming from artists' exploration of non-representational art (Islamic culture is aniconistic), these patterns, which are often used together, can be found drawn and painted, pierced and embossed, woven and carved onto walls, doors, floors, ceilings, ceramics and textiles right across the Islamic world from Morocco to Malaysia.

The intricate geometric designs most often associated with Islamic patterns are rooted in classical Greek and Roman forms, such as circles and squares, which are then duplicated, interlaced and overlapped until they form exquisitely complex kaleidoscopes of pattern. Fascinating and pulse quickening, the designs are based on unity and order, which means they are also fabulously easy to live with.

Symmetry is fundamental to harmonious design, exemplifying perfection and satisfying our desire to find order in chaos. Symmetry is also fundamental to the patterns of the Islamic world, which is why they can be used on a grand scale – just think of the Alhambra. And, as these two interiors show, total immersion works in domestic spaces too.

Above: Both pretty and orderly, this tight-repeat pattern inspired by geometric Islamic motifs makes a decorative backdrop for this modern bedroom. The shape of the lampshade draws attention to the motif's form, while the bright cushion adds an energizing pop of visual contrast.

Opposite: The motifs on this wallpaper tessellate across the surface with such an even rhythm that the effect is both mesmerizing and rather soothing. Repeating the pattern on the lampshades and cushions brings it off the wall and into the room, creating a sense of depth. The narrow stripes on the sofa add a flash of contrast that brings the scheme to life. Design: Susi Bellamy.

CULTURAL TRAVELLERS

Richly patterned and coloured tiles are a feature of many countries of the Islamic world. Follow their lead and use them on walls and floors, inside and out.

Opposite: Floors are wonderful vehicles for pattern, especially in spaces where you don't want the pattern to dominate. (Unlike walls, you don't look directly at floors.) Here, the richly patterned tiles are offset by a subtle pink-striped wall to create an eclectic, multi-cultural look that is totally twenty-first century.

Above Left: Cultural influences abound in this sitting room, from the intricate Islamic-patterned wall tiles to the plaid upholstery on the armchair. The elements that bring it all together are the underlying geometry and repeated flashes of yellow.

Above Right: Running the tiles over the floor and up onto the wall means that this sparsely furnished kitchen is enveloped in pattern. The way the tiles have been arranged on the wall adds another element of interest to the design.

Pops of pattern can come from all manner of sources, from pouffes sourced in a Moroccan bazaar to bed linen and balustrades.

Above Left: A bold rug will bring a space to life. Here, the stitching on the two leather pouffes and the monochrome flower pot bring the pattern off the floor and into the room, creating a more immersive look that doesn't overwhelm.
Design: Graham and Green.

Above Right: In this bedroom, stripes and Islamic-inspired geometric forms have been set one against the other. The large scale of the stripe balances the bold pattern on the bed, while a pair of pillows printed with just the outline shape introduces another layer of visual interest.

Opposite: Decorative architectural features are a good way to inject an element of pattern into pared-down interiors. The regular geometry of this balustrade creates a sense of movement that leads the eye up, or down, the stairs.

SCENES & STORIES

Textile and wallpaper designers have a long history of using their chosen materials as canvases for pictures. The simplest feature realistic images of objects, figures or animals, while many others depart from traditional pattern making, embracing instead the decorative power of the continuous scene. The following pages show the vast range of styles on offer, from traditional toile de Jouy and chinoiserie to digitally printed dresses and trompe l'oeil landscapes.

Opposite: The vast mountain scene is given free reign in this space. The undulating shapes of the simple modern furniture reflect the lines of the landscape behind, while a tufted rug adds a welcome note of warmth.

PANORAMAS

Whether it's a breathtaking mountain view, a tranquil woodland glade or an exciting night-time cityscape filled with bright lights and big rooftops, digital printing has enabled us to bring the outside world right into our homes. Have you always wanted to live by waterfalls in Thailand? No problem, a wall mural company near you will be happy to oblige. The large scale of many of these scenic wallpapers and fabrics does make them more challenging to accommodate than other forms of pattern, but they also allow us to construct new realities within our own homes, and that is a very exciting prospect indeed. Of course, the absence of a repeat means these scenic creations are not patterns at all in the strictest sense, but they are so full of different shapes and colours and forms that the effect is much the same. Plain they are not.

The technology might be new, but the idea that decoration can provide a window to the world, either as it really is or as the artist would like it to be, dates back thousands of years. Think of tapestries. In the eleventh century, the Bayeux Tapestry told the story of the events leading up to the Norman conquest of England, while 300 years later, workshops in Flanders were producing a steady stream of tapestries depicting idealized pastoral landscapes for royalty, merchants and landowners to hang in their homes.

But it was the increasing sophistication of wallpaper-manufacturing processes in the early nineteenth century that led to the explosion of interest in scenic decorating. France led the way, keen to challenge the popularity of English flock papers. These 'Papiers Peint-Paysages', as they were known, depicted either mythological and historic events like the destruction of Pompeii, or exotic landscapes inspired by French colonies such as Senegal or Cambodia. Designed to be wrapped around entire rooms, these papers created a continuous and immersive panoramic effect.

As a craze, panorama-mania was intense but short-lived. Few people had homes large enough to accommodate papers of such scale and fewer still could afford to pay the high prices they commanded. Fortunately, for contemporary fans of the style, technology has substantially reduced the cost of doing up your living room in a 360-degree recreation of the Swiss Alps, but scenes like this demand our attention in ways that conventional repeating patterns do not, so they need to be handled with care. The secret, as the following pictures show, is to let them take centre stage.

Outside might be all concrete and cars, but inside you can be in Arcadia.

Above Left: Here, a wall-sized mural of a woodland envelops an otherwise empty hallway. The wooden floor helps to connect the physical space to the virtual one. Featureless spaces such as halls and landings make perfect canvases for panoramic designs and if you can do without furniture, so much the better. However, if a piece or two is necessary, try to keep it below eye level so as not to spoil the view.

Above Right: Rather than let the opulent garden scene take the spotlight, as is usual with panoramics, the designer behind this extravagant sitting room has used it as a backdrop for layer upon layer of other patterns. The result is certainly full on, but it works because, despite ignoring the centre-stage guideline, the scheme does follow the rules about mixing patterns. Every pattern here shares a common botanical theme, the colour palette is limited to yellow and green and the motifs come in a variety of scales. Design: Mindthegap.

Above Left: Panoramic wallpapers are like paintings and in this scheme the paper has been hung so that the scene is framed by the architecture of the landing. The plain, bold colours of the rooms on either side enliven the muted tones of the wallpaper.

Above Right: What could be more conducive to a good night's sleep than a bedroom wall transformed into a skyscape of dreamy clouds? The soft, organic shapes of the clouds also make a good backdrop for the mix of geometric patterns on the bed.

For a sharper, chicer take on panoramics, try a sweeping cityscape. Keep the colour scheme black and white, the furniture simple, add a metallic flash and you're done.

Top Left: Panoramic wallpapers allow you to play with perspective – here, the eye is drawn out of the room and on into the Venetian scene beyond, making the room feel larger. The stripes on the curtain and radiator pick up on the lines of brickwork in the scene and add a second layer of pattern.

Bottom Left: A large-scale city panorama makes a dramatic backdrop to this glamorous but minimally furnished dining room. As with the previous scheme, bringing a grand view into the room makes the space feel far bigger – and more interesting – than it really is.

Opposite: This is the city panorama as pattern rather than picture. Hung as a single panel, as in this photograph, it makes a big, painting-like statement but the density of the imagery means that, on a large scale, individual buildings and rooftops merge, creating a subtler, more textural effect.

TROMPE L'OEIL

Trompe l'oeil is a technique that uses realistic imagery to create the optical illusion that the landscape, people or object depicted exists in three dimensions. A huge hit in eighteenth-century France when friezes imitating drapery fought for space against virtual vistas, they are now back in fashion thanks to the wonders of digital printing. Witty, trippy and space shifting, trompe l'oeil decorating has the power to transform your interior.

Opposite: It's the classical statuary that first catches your eye in this imitation of a Roman villa, but it is the geometry of the surrounding architecture that makes the design so effective as a pattern. Combining straight lines and curving arches, it gives the room a sense of grandeur, while the three-dimensional quality of the trompe l'oeil adds depth, creating a sense of space. Design: Mindthegap.

Right: In both these schemes, a wall of trompe l'oeil bookshelves has been used to create an inviting sitting area within a large, open-plan space. Both interiors are rather pared down and contemporary, so the geometric shape of the shelves and books is an effective way of introducing some pattern.

In the top image, the oblong shape of each individual section of the bookcase reflects, in a slightly larger scale, the brickwork on the adjoining wall. The wood floor and ceiling add a contrasting striped element. Bottom: Design: Deborah Bowness.

CHINOISERIE

Chinoiserie is a decorative style inspired by the art and design of Asian countries, chiefly Japan and China (the name comes from 'chinois', the French for Chinese), that was imported into Europe in the eighteenth century by the East India Trading Company. Chief amongst these imports were Chinese wallpapers, exquisitely hand-painted papers featuring large-scale, non-repeating pictorial scenes of either day-to-day Chinese life (farmers working in the paddy fields were a common theme), or landscapes filled with unfamiliar plants and birds. The exoticism of the imagery, combined with a level of detail and quality of colour unrivalled by any Western-made wallpapers meant that these 'China papers' soon became the wall covering of choice for the wealthy and fashionable in both Europe and the United States. And so they remained for much of the rest of the century, particularly for bedrooms, drawing and dining rooms where the delicate informality of the style could be fully appreciated.

The nineteenth and twentieth centuries were not kind to chinoiserie (aside from a brief period in the 1920s), but the recent return to more decorative interiors has led to a comeback. Beautifully ornate and less obviously scenic than the panoramic papers of the previous pages, chinoiserie is surprisingly timeless.

Chinoiserie was originally designed for use on all four walls, so follow the lead of those eighteenth-century taste-makers and discover the joys of immersive pattern.

Opposite: Rather than take the chinoiserie wall-to-wall, in this room it has been paired with other more abstracted, geometric patterns. The result is a jewel box of a space that might be hard to live with, let alone sleep in, were it not for the strict colour scheme and close attention to the scale of each motif. Look carefully and you will see large, medium and small motifs have been carefully placed one against the other throughout the room, creating a calming sense of balance.

Above Left: A delicate blue chinoiserie wallpaper wraps the walls of this classically designed bedroom, forming a quiet backdrop for the more densely patterned fabric on the bedhead. The rug introduces a cleaner, more geometric note to balance the flowing central pattern, and also brings the various colours used in the room together.

Above Right: Clean modernity and decorative tradition combine here. The chinoiserie design brings movement and interest to the space, softening all the straight lines and hard materials. The design also suggests a pretty garden, which, since this is a basement, is a welcome reminder of the natural world. Design: Fromental.

It may not have been designed for the feature wall, but used over a small area, chinoiserie really sings. This is wallpaper as statement artwork.

Above Left: Here, a large-scale chinoiserie design has been used to turn a hallway into a highly decorative room in its own right. The scrolling horizontal repeat on the border acts as a frame and also balances the flowing vertical lines of the trees below.

Above Right: Chinoiserie can never be minimal, but it can be more restrained as this image shows. Lots of white space between each motif gives the eye places to rest and the simplified motifs lower the tempo.

Opposite: In this bedroom, the richly patterned headboard and matching cushions bring the pattern off the wall and into the room itself, adding to the sense of luxury. Design: Watts of Westminster.

Still not sure such ornate prettiness is for your walls? There are other ways to bring a touch of chinoiserie magic into your homes.

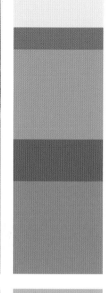

Opposite: Keeping the walls plain and using the furniture to introduce accents of pattern into predominately plain schemes is a trick often used by interior decorators. In this bedroom, the soft lines of the trees on the cupboard are balanced by the sharper lines of the floorboards. Both lead the eye up, seeming to raise the height of the ceiling.

Top Right: This scheme demonstrates how well the motifs of chinoiserie, in this case trailing branches of blossom, work with more structured patterns such as ikat.

Bottom Right: Chinoiserie designs can be found adorning all kinds of decorative accessories from table lamps to tableware. Seek some out (vintage stores and charity shops are a good, inexpensive source), gather them all together in a perfectly co-ordinated set or a riot of assorted patterns and display as a tableau.

Opposite: Printed with repeated vignettes, this toile wallpaper appears utterly traditional, but closer inspection reveals that the scenes are, in fact, gritty depictions of contemporary London. In this scheme, that juxtaposition of traditional and modern is reflected in the way the paper has been used a backdrop for a very twenty-first century staircase and lighting system. Design: Timorous Beasties.

TOILE DE JOUY

Literally translated, toile de Jouy means 'cloth from the town of Jouy'. The cloth is cotton, and Jouy, or Jouy en Jouas to give it its full title, is a small town not far from Paris where, in 1760, Christophe-Philippe Oberkampf opened a cotton-printing factory.

A year earlier, the French King Louis XV had lifted a ban on the importation of Indian cotton (imposed to boost native wool and silk industries), and Oberkampf spotted an opportunity. He wasn't the only one – Europe was obsessed with Indian cotton at this time – but the toiles his factory produced were exceptional. Printed with engraved copper plates rather than wooden blocks, they allowed for an almost three-dimensional level of detail and a much larger repeat. Oberkampf exploited these qualities to the full, commissioning some of the best artists of the day to create pictorial narratives reflecting historic events such as the first hot-air balloon flight, oriental landscapes and, most famously of all, vignettes of bucolic pastoral scenes in which shepherdesses minded their flocks and gentle folk gathered beneath leaf-full trees.

These fabrics swiftly became the toast of eighteenth-century French nobility – Louis XVI and Marie Antoinette were enthusiastic fans – and, without copyright laws to protect Oberkampf's designs, it wasn't long before other factories were producing replicas, not just on cotton but on wallpaper too. Wider availability and lower costs spread the popularity of toile to England and America, where designs celebrated everything from the American Revolution to home-grown heroes such as Tom Sawyer and Benjamin Franklin.

In the eighteenth century, toile de Jouy was used to cover entire rooms – walls, curtains and all. Contemporary toiles, of which there are many, tend to be used on a smaller scale, more as central features than background decoration. With themes ranging from classic country landscapes to edgier urban scenes and a largely monochrome colour palette (the first toiles were printed on the natural white of the cotton and the scenes painted on top in a single colour, often red, blue or violet), there is a toile du Jouy to suit every style of interior.

With its pretty, pastoral vignettes and delicate colourways, toile de Jouy was made for the bedroom.

Above Left: The bed is the star attraction in this room. Its simple, contemporary shape allows for a generous mix of patterns and colours – red toile de Jouy sits beneath a large embroidered grey leaf motif, which rests against blue pinstriped cushions. The white walls and white sheets allow each separate pattern space to breathe.

Above Right: This bedroom confines the toile de Jouy to a single chest at the end of the bed where it becomes a focal point. The only other pattern in the room comes from the geometric arrangement of the pictures on the wall, the straight lines neatly balancing the softer forms of the toile.

Above Left: Toile de Jouy was made for use on all four
walls and across curtains and upholstery too, just as it's
seen in this attic bedroom. (Running it over the ceiling is
a very twenty-first century touch.) Full-on co-ordination is a
bold look, but as this image proves, it is also wonderfully
cocooning. Keep furniture sparse and simple and avoid any
other forms of decoration. The vignettes alone are enough.

Above Right: The flouncy romance of the fabric and
canopy are countered in this French-flavoured bedroom by
the edgier blrown-and-white colour palette. The parquet
floor and a finely patterned rug introduce additional layers
of pattern which balance the scheme.

Bathrooms were made for pattern – often small and viewless, they need to be dressed up. Toile de Jouy may not be traditional for a bathroom, but the delicacy of the pattern is a good way to bring a note of softness to what can be rather hard, functional spaces.

Above: Romance meets geometry in this bathroom where a pretty pastoral toile is matched with a square-tiled wall and diamond-patterned floor. The result lifts the spirits.

Opposite: A delicate blue toile de Jouy is perfectly suited to this traditional bathroom. The pretty romance of the classic toile motif is reflected in small flashes of additional pattern such as the decorative carving on the top of the cabinet and the ornate frame around the mirror.

Toile de Jouy looks wonderful used on a large scale, as the previous pages show, but that doesn't mean it can't work small. Because the patterns are composed of individual vignettes, they can be shrunk to fit. Think sofas, cushions and even vintage bowls.

Opposite: Even a quiet reading area benefits from a dose of pattern. This toile de Jouy-covered armchair, teamed with a check cushion, adds visual interest without detracting from the sense of calm.

Top Right: Ticking and toile de Jouy are a perfect match. The gentle stripe balances the bold pattern and also allows it to take centre stage.

Bottom Right: Dress up your dinner table with some pretty toile de Jouy. Team with plain crockery and linen as in this picture, or mix with as many other patterns as you can lay your hands on. Use the table as an experimental canvas. After all, it's easy to change if it all goes wrong.

REPEATING PICTURES

The simplest of all picture-based patterns are those that take a realistic image – animal, vegetable, mineral – and use it again and again to cover a surface. The repeat makes these patterns easy to use in domestic spaces, and the fact that they are made up of recognizable things means they attract our attention in a way that other patterns do not.

Above and Opposite: The repeat is central to the success of both of these patterns, turning simple pictures of domestic objects into rhythmic patterns soothing enough to run across entire walls. Above: Design: Mini Moderns. Opposite: Design: Tracy Kendall.

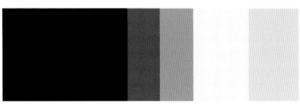

We are drawn to look at faces so if you want your walls to attract attention, try covering them in a people-based pattern.

Above Left: Faces jump out at us. Repeated circles create a soothing rhythm. Put the two together and you get a very successful pattern indeed.

Above Right: This kaleidoscopic pattern plays games with our sense of perspective and creates a three-dimensional effect, which would add depth to a small space. Design: Identity Papers.

Opposite: A closed repeat of cameo portraits wraps all four walls in this playful recreation of a Victorian drawing room. It is intentionally busy, as was the fashion at the time, but the dark colour of the paper and plenty of white accents (courtesy of the chairs, curtain and fireplace) do allow the eye an occasional resting place.

Opposite: This paper has a lovely, flowing rhythm thanks to the alternating shapes and scales of the paper lantern motifs. The floral decoration on each one adds a decorative element that brings the pattern to life. Design: Mini Moderns.

Top Right: Part repeating image, part trompe l'oeil, this mural makes a witty backdrop to a breakfast bar. The straight rows formed by the shelves also inject some subtle pattern into an otherwise plain white space.

Bottom Right: Here, a wall of book covers injects a pop of colour and life into a hallway. The band of white that runs through each row gives the eye a path to follow, which helps to anchor the pattern.

ANIMAL KINGDOM

———

Animal skins have been used to clothe both our bodies and our homes throughout history, while the instinct to draw, paint, weave and carve depictions of the creatures who share our world connects human cultures across place and time. A bull is the subject of what is thought to be the world's oldest cave painting, made some 40,000 years ago. In the Middle Ages animals, both real and imagined, were used to ornament everything from jewellery to cooking pots and sacred texts, while in the eighteenth century, the butterflies, golden pheasants and three-clawed dragons of ancient Chinese textiles became the decorating motifs of choice amongst Europe's fashionable and influential elite. In modern times, animal-based patterns are most often found decorating children's rooms, while the prints inspired by animal skins have suffered from an association with 1970s kitsch. But, as the following pages prove, the animal kingdom has much more to offer pattern lovers than cuddly bears and zebra-striped plush settees.

Left: The wall of pink flamingos injects real joy into this bathroom. It makes you smile but it is more elegant than kitsch, an effect that is entirely due to the clever use of pattern. The formal geometry of the wood panelling and broad-striped floor not only allows the flamingos to shine, it also draws attention to the underlying structure of the pattern on the wall. The motif is big and bright, but it occurs in repeat so it develops a sense of rhythm as you look at it.

Opposite: Geometric patterns have been used to ground the flamboyant flamingos (and other exotic birds) in this bathroom too. In this case, the paper itself has a graphic diamond background, which creates a depth-enhancing, three-dimensional effect. The mirror is a neat trick – the reflection reinforces the grid-like pattern that provides the framework for the scheme, while its round shape is a pop of contrast.
Design: Divine Savages.

ANIMAL MOTIFS

Pictures of animals have always carried meaning. According to the medieval bestiaries (vast compendiums containing illustrations of all manner of actual and mythological creatures and the morals they represented), lions symbolized strength and vigilance, pelicans signified charity, and griffins stood as guardians for the dead, while in ancient Mayan culture, open-winged butterflies represented freedom. Today, the original symbolism of the animal motifs we use to decorate our homes have been overlaid with other, more contemporary interpretations. In the schemes on these pages, for example, pink flamingos – a symbol of the Ancient Egyptian sun god Ra and a familiar motif in the art deco architecture of 1920s Miami – have been used as shorthand for summer, glamour and good times.

These schemes demonstrate that animal motifs can be chic, sophisticated and the very essence of grown-up elegance.

Opposite: Placed on a dark background, butterflies take on a sophisticated and glamorous look. The variety of scales used across the repeat gives the paper a sense of depth and texture.

Above Left: A single wall covered in a pattern of birds in flight brings a sense of movement to this tiny galley kitchen, which is echoed in the flowing floral motif on the wall tiles. Confining the paper to such a small area turns it into a real feature, more artwork than decoration. Design: Daniel Heath Studio.

Above Right: Here, a rich jungle scene, in which monkeys cling to fruit-laden trees, is framed within a series of arched wall panels, drawing attention to the imagery. The undulating rhythm of the architecture reflects the sinuous lines of the wallpaper design.

Printed small and in tight, closed repeats, animal motifs make surprisingly quiet, almost textural, backdrops that are perfect for bedrooms. They are particularly popular for decorating children's rooms – a sign perhaps that we still hold on to the idea that animals can be friendly companions and wise teachers of moral lessons.

Above Left: This is a bright and busy pattern, but the small scale of the motif means that the pattern recedes on a large wall. Repeating the scale in the abstract patterns on the cushions enhances the textual impression of this scheme.

Above Right: Children's bedrooms should be full of fun and visual interest, but the atmosphere needs to be calm and conducive to sleep. Depicting horses in motion and arranging them in regular rows gives this pattern a lovely sense of rhythm.

Opposite: A wall of long-eared rabbits might not sound like a very soothing, or stylish, form of decoration but rendered in black and white and drawn in such tight repeat that they almost overlap, the pattern turns into texture, and it is only when you get close that the motif really reveals itself. The patina of the metal chest of drawers and visible grain on the wooden floor add two further layers of visual texture.

Right: Here, a pair of zebra-print armchairs mixes with a floral rug and a scattering of geometric cushions, creating a richly decorative but totally cohesive scheme. Plain dark walls frame the layers of pattern within the room, while the single stripe on the curtains provides a visual link between the two. Design: Lisa Gilmore Design.

ANIMAL PRINTS

Time was when animal prints meant real hides – in the Victorian age, bringing the outside in meant covering the floor with the skins of exotic game (as well as furnishing the walls with stuffed heads) as a sign of your well-travelled sophistication. In the 1920s and 1930s, when the first professional interior designers arrived on the scene, they started a fashion for mixing animal prints with chinoiserie and eighteenth-century antiques. The leader of the look was Elsie de Wolfe, who ran a zebra-print runner down the stairs of actress Hope Hampton's otherwise classically furnished Park Avenue apartment.

The 1960s and 1970s saw animal prints move from accents to focal points, with real and replica skins used to cover everything from floors and walls to sofas and beds. Was it the over use of satin leopard-print sheets that led to the look's eventual fall from fashion? Perhaps. But in today's world, animal prints are far sleeker and more sophisticated than their seventies cousins (nor do they cause any harm to the creatures who inspire them), so it's time to embrace the patterns of the animal kingdom once more and take a walk on the wild side.

We tend to think animal skin-inspired patterns should be allowed to stand alone as the only pattern in a scheme, but dare to mix them with other patterns and you will discover they have a much quieter and more discreet side too, blending into their surroundings like a leopard in the grasses.

Opposite: This gloriously patterned dining room brings out the camouflage potential of animal print to the full. On its own, this cheetah-print chair would take centre stage; set against florals and geometrics, it simply adds a note of visual texture.

Top Right: This bedroom is a celebration of visual texture. The leopard-print bed linen (the twenty-first century version is a great deal chicer than its 1970s counterpart) is so densely patterned that it almost disappears against the woven patterns of the surrounding fabrics.

Bottom Right: This elegant and contemporary sitting room shows that animal prints really can work anywhere. The zebra-print rug and chaise add a touch of drama and glamour, but they don't shout for attention because the dense pattern reads as texture. And that means it can mix happily with both the sharp geometry of the hexagon-print floor tiles and those delicate florals on the doors.

Of course, for every discreet leopard there is a displaying peacock. Occasional and transitional spaces such as cloakrooms, landings and hallways are made for statement decorating because you don't spend much time in them and, since they only serve a single function, they generally don't require too much in the way of furniture.

Above: Nothing says 'nightclub glamour' like animal prints and glossy surfaces. The large scale of the zebra print on the floor next to the smaller, cheetah-inspired wall, gives the scheme depth and richness.

Opposite: Land and sea collide in this small but statement-making cloakroom. At first glance, the bold zebra stripe might seem an odd choice of flooring given the nautical theme, but look again and you will notice that the markings echo the outlines of the continents on the map covering the walls. That visual connection is the reason the room works.

The previous pages showed how well animal prints mix with other patterns. The interiors here celebrate the drama of a single statement.

Above Left: Even the most minimal of interiors can accommodate some animal pattern. In this scheme, the colours have been kept muted and natural, emphasizing the visual texture created by the close stripes of the zebra print so as not to disturb the calm serenity of the room.

Above Right: This room in contrast is bright and white, allowing the pattern to take centre stage. Without the zebra print it would be cold, flat and featureless; with it, it sings.

Above Left: Stairs are a wonderful canvas for pattern. The lines of this zebra print draw the eye up to the roof light. The wooden floor and ordered arrangement of pictures on the back wall provide additional layers of geometric pattern, giving the minimally furnished and white-walled space a sense of depth and interest.

Above Right: The leopard-print headboard brings this white bedroom to life. The texture of the painted brickwork draws attention to the apparent texture of pattern and the small pops of print in the corner of the room help to give the scheme a sense of balance.

TEXTURES

When interior designers talk about texture, they are referring to the surface
quality of a material. Smooth, rough, hard or soft, every surface has a texture
of some sort that can be used, like colour and pattern, to add interest, depth
and personality to a room. But why include it in a book about pattern? The
answer is all around you, from the bubble wrap protecting your latest online
purchase to corrugated iron, the bark on the tree outside, the cracked bed of
a dried-out river, a reptile's scales and the wind-blown ridges of sand dunes.
As all these natural and man-made things show, textures carry pattern within
them. The following pages are full of beautiful rooms filled with textural
pattern – read on and be inspired.

TACTILE TEXTURE

Tactile texture is a physical thing. Produced by the surface quality of the material, it refers to how something actually feels when we touch it. These sensations elicit certain responses (the softness of a woollen blanket makes us feel cosy and safe, for example), which can be used to create different moods. Fill a room with raised textures and you get warm, relaxed, rural. Opt for smooth – a polished concrete floor, shiny metallic details on the furniture, silk-covered cushions – and the look is instantly cooler, sleeker and more urban. Strip off the plaster to expose a raw brick wall and you have instant industrial chic.

Many of these tactile materials can be found in the existing architectural details of our homes, such as brick or plaster walls and tiled floors, while others can be introduced with furniture and decorative accessories. Look for woven textiles and natural materials with a grain. Remember too that bumpy surfaces have peaks and valleys, which allow you to play with light and shadow, enhancing their pattern potential even more.

Top Left: This indoor/outdoor living space combines both visual and tactile pattern. The brick floor has been laid in a herringbone pattern, which instantly creates a sense of warmth, despite the hard surfaces. The wicker chairs echo the weave pattern on the floor and add depth to the scheme.

Bottom Left: Pattern is to the fore in this hallway, but there's not a printed pattern to be seen; the effect is created entirely through the structural materials. Smooth slate floor slabs sit against a rough brick wall, the sharp contrast creating interest and energizing the space.

Opposite: This peeling plaster wall is a perfect example of wabi-sabi, the Japanese idea of finding beauty in imperfection. The patina of the various materials creates an appealing, tactile pattern that turns the wall into a feature in its own right. Design: Mark Alexander.

Textural patterns are subtler than their printed cousins, but you still need to think about the visual effect they have on a room. Like pattern, texture can alter our perception of scale. Just as horizontal and vertical lines direct our gaze, so too do textures with directional grain or weaves, making spaces appear taller or wider. Rough textures can also seem to reduce the scale of objects, so if your sofa is too visually dominating, try covering it in knobbly wool.

Opposite: This sitting room shows how physical texture can be used to bring interest and character to serene and minimal interiors. Natural materials such as wood and raffia combine with woven upholstery fabric, its lines neatly reflecting those in the ceiling and lampshade. Design: Mark Alexander.

Above Left: Furniture is a great vehicle for tactile pattern. The bumpy, woven surface of this wicker chair would bring a sense of geometry and warmth to any room.

Above Right: Lining the wall with rough-cut wooden planks not only gives this room a sense of rustic, upcycled chic, it also creates a focal point. Painting the planks in a variety of toning colours draws attention to the vertical stripe.

Wallpaper and tiles are more usually associated with printed pattern, but as the following images show, they can also be used to fill rooms with tactile delight too.

Above Left: A wall of embossed metal tiles makes an unusual and striking feature in this bedroom. Metal is a cold material, but here it is countered by the tactility of the embossed pattern. The decorative nature of the motif also helps to soften the industrial feel of the material.

Above Right: This wallpaper is composed of individual leaves of paper, hand-stitched onto a backing sheet. The result is so full of visual and physical texture (encounter it in real life and you won't be able to resist running your hands down it), that it doesn't need colour or printed pattern to attract attention, making it the perfect choice for minimal homes. Design: Tracy Kendall.

Opposite: These ceramic wall tiles not only ask to be touched, they also bring a three-dimensional element to the room, giving it a real sense of depth. The hard, shiny surface of the glazed ceramic offset by the bumpy tactility of the relief and the fluffy warmth of the rug and cushion results in a scheme that appeals to all the senses. Design: Jonathan Adler.

The texture of a surface influences the quality of light in a room. Smooth surfaces are reflective, so will make colours appear sharper and spaces larger. Rough, matt surfaces, on the other hand, absorb the light, deepening colours and drawing in walls. Both are good looks, but you need to decide what mood you want to create.

Top Left: Textured wallpapers date back to the nineteenth century when they were used on ceilings and the lower sections of walls to imitate decorative plasterwork. Production techniques and styles have moved on, but the effect is the same – relief papers bring instant depth, definition and warmth to your walls. Here, a dramatic black paper with a slightly raised surface creates a luxurious, tactile backdrop for the statement bed.

Bottom Left: Three-dimensional motifs draw your attention in a way that flat patterns do not, inviting you to get close and to interact. Here, the wall with its raised circles becomes a part of the mantlepiece display, rather than simply a decorative backdrop.

Opposite: This mural of meadow grasses has been cast in plaster, turning it into a three-dimensional piece of wall art that invites you to touch it. The slight roughness of the plaster is a nice contrast to the smoothness of the wood floor and panelling. Design: Rachel Dein.

VISUAL TEXTURE

Visual texture is an illusion. Rather than being physically cold or warm, hard or soft, bumpy or smooth to the touch, visually textured surfaces give the impression of these sensations. We know marble feels cold, we know wool and wood are warm, so when we see something that looks as if it is made from these materials, we make assumptions about how they will feel to the touch. Those assumptions are such powerful things that if you fill a room with lots of warm-looking surfaces then, while it may not actually raise your temperature, being in it will certainly be a cosy experience.

Above: A wall of different geometric tiles brings a richly textural feel to this scheme. There are several different patterns here, but the dark tones and regular geometry ensure visual harmony, while the rough wooden shelf adds a layer of physical texture. Design: Daniel Heath Studio.

Opposite: This wall might look as though it is covered in a mosaic of carved bronze tiles, but if you were to walk over and touch it – which you would – you'd find that the surface is not only flat but also made of painted paper. The apparent three-dimensionality of this wallpaper gives the space depth and fills it with pattern, while the visual trickery of the trompe l'oeil is a clever, witty surprise. Design: Fromental.

Wood is warm and connects us to the natural world. Its veins and markings are also patterns in their own right. All these images embrace the wonders of the faux wood wall.

Opposite and Above Left: These schemes celebrate the artificiality of wood-effect pattern. The sense of the warming texture of real wood comes through and the oversized wood grain adds visual depth, but there's a lovely playful element here too which makes these happy spaces to live in. Opposite: Design: Kirill Istomin.

Above Right: Here, a subtle and realistic wood-effect paper has been used to create a mid-century feel. The horizontal grain adds width to the room and balances the vertical lines of the other patterns.

Wallpapers that look like fabrics are another way to bring subtle pattern and a sense of texture to a room and, since just looking at highly textured fabric makes us feel warm, they are perfect for cocooning spaces such as bedrooms and studies.

Opposite: The guidelines around mixing pattern advise layering in odd numbers. There are four layers of printed pattern in this bedroom (duvet cover, pillows, cushions and lampshades), so using a wallpaper that reads more as texture for the fifth is a good way to ensure balance without pattern overload.

Top Right: The check repeat on this wallpaper is so small that it looks like woven tweed. Wrapping it around all four walls turns this functional office space into something altogether prettier and more domestic. The paper is also a perfect backdrop for the framed artwork because the small scale of the check allows the larger, more rounded motifs to stand out.

Bottom Right: This wall is a clever play on the upholstered headboard. It also brings a real sense of softness to the room, despite the cool colour scheme.

Above: This bedroom is full of textural pattern, both physical and visual, and the interest comes from the way the scheme plays with our perceptions. The wallpaper looks like marble, which is rather cold to the touch, but the wiggling organic lines give it a softness which, matched by the thick pile of the rug, creates a luxurious sense of warmth. Design: Natasha Baradaran.

Opposite: This scheme makes the most of the power of suggestion. The wall is rigid, smooth and hard to the touch, but because it depicts a meadow of head-high grasses, it fills the room with a sense of softness and movement. So rich is the visual experience that no other pattern is required.

INDEX

V

W

Y

Z

FURTHER READING

Books for curious eyes and minds:

Pantone History of Colour by Leatrice Eiseman & Keith Recker (Chronicle Books, 2011)

Pattern Design by Elizabeth Wilhide (Thames & Hudson, 2018) & US version, *The Complete Pattern Directory: 1500 Designs from all Ages & Cultures* (Hachette USA)

Patternalia: An Unconventional History of Polka Dots, Stripes, Plaid, Camouflage & other Graphic Patterns by Jude Stewart (Bloomsbury, 2015)

Patternity: A New Way of Seeing: The Inspirational Power of Pattern by Patternity (Conran, 2015)

The Little Book of Colour: How to use the psychology of colour to transform your life by Karen Haller (Penguin Life, 2019)

The Secret Lives of Colour by Kassia St Clair (John Murray, 2018)

20th Century Pattern Design: Textile & Wallpaper Pioneers by Lesley Jackson (Mitchell Beazley, 2011)

ONLINE INSPIRATION

Websites to check out; these all have great Instagram accounts too:

Apartmenttherapy.com US & UK home and decor site, designed to inspire anyone to live a more beautiful and happy life at home.

Decorbydelali.uk UK-based, colour-loving interior designer with inspiration-led blog and Instagram.

JonathanAdler.com US brand. The website has US & UK sites with inspiration-led blog.

Jungalow.com US-based design blog and lifestyle brand with a mission to inspire creativity.

MadAbouttheHouse.com UK-based award-winning interior design blog described as a 'source book for modern living'.

Patternity.org UK-based 'Conscious Creative Organisation' and lifestyle brand conceived to share the positive power of pattern with the world.

Patternspy.com UK-based resource for anyone planning a decorating scheme.

SophieRobinson.co.uk British interior designer Sophie Robinson is known as the 'undisputed colour queen'. Her blog is full of inspiring home decorating ideas.

SwoonWorthy.co.uk UK-based, award-winning interior design and DIY blog. The Home of Eclectic Boho Glam.

Thespruce.com US-based home decorating brand.

WhitneyJdecor.com US-based interior designer with inspiration-led blog.

PICTURE CREDITS

123 Wallpaper – 'Mr Chrysanth' by Abigail Borg/Photographer – Laura Edwards; 124 t Getty Images/Tom Kelley Archive; 124 b Living4Media/Rebecca Martyn; 125 Tracy Kendall/Photographer Ollie Harrop; 126 Living4Media/Tim Imrie; 127 Getty Images/thierrydehove.com; 128 Fabric/cushion/lampshade – 'Feverfew Midnight' by Abigail Borg. Photo credit : Francesca Stone.; 129 Living4Media/Annette Nordstrom; 130 l Living4Media/Syl Loves; 130 r Living4Media/Martin Sølyst; 131 l Living4Media/Great Stock; 131 r Mindthegap Ottoman anthracite wallpaper, sofa in Gypsy Ochre linen www.mindtheg.com; 132 Getty Images/Vostok; 134 Living4Media/Andreas von Einsiedel; 135 Living4Media/Cecilia Möller; 136 MissPrint Frontier Flint Wallpaper, priced at £76.00 per roll (10m x 52cm) www.missprint.co.uk; 137 l Arcaid/Richard Powers; 137 r Cloud Rococo Ombre Wallpaper, Happy Blue, by Identity Papers; 138 Interior: Kate Watson-Smyth of madabouthehouse.com, Runner: Waterlake by Ella Doran for Alternative Flooring, Made from British Wool inspired by The Yorkshire Sculpture Park.; 139 Hula Swirl Noir, £55 per roll, Graham & Brown x Barbara Hulanicki; 140 l Getty Images/Vostok; 140 r Wallcovering: Fromental – Ponti in colourway Planchard. Designer: Maddux Creative. Photo: David Jensen; 141 l Designers Guild Suisai Celadon Wallpaper PDG1114/01; 141 r Getty Images/ExperienceInteriors; 142 Andreas von Einsiedel/Alamy Stock Photo; 143 Living4Media/Christoph Theurer; 144 Living4Media/Nicolas Bouriette; 145 Living4Media/Stuart Cox; 146 l Getty Images/ExperienceInteriors; 146 r MELT Wallcovering in Dawn Colorway by Jill Malek, for State Bird Provisions in San Francisco, photographed by Sydney Brown; 147 REFLECTIONS Wallcovering by Jill Malek in Moonlit Colorway.; 148 Amelia Graham; 150 Scarpa Gelim in France 2016, Hand dyed and woven flatweave rug, wool. Made in India designed by Ptolemy Mann/Manufactured by Rugmaker. Photo: Chris McCourt; 151 Indigo Ochre Gelim in 2018, Hand dyed and woven flatweave rug, wool. Made in India designed by Ptolemy Mann/Manufactured by Rugmaker. Photo: Katya de Grunwald; 152 Fabrics by Manuel Canovas. Manuel Canovas at Colefax and Fowler; 153 l GAP Photos/Caruth Studio; 153 r GAP Interiors/Costas Picadas; 154 Getty Images/David Papazian; 155 Living4Media/View Pictures; 156 Mindthegap Yoruba wallpaper www.mindtheg.com; 157 t Amelia Graham for Sunbury Design/Photographer Stephen Belcher; 157 b Mindthegap Bamana wallpaper www.mindtheg.com; 158–159 Amelia Graham/Photographer Taran Wilkhu/Studio 2LG; 160 t Living4Media/Matteo Manduzio; 160 b RE, 01434 634567, www.re-foundobjects.com; 161 Living4Media/N.Zweig/T.Roch; 162 PR Shots/Debenhams; 163 Living4Media/Matteo Manduzio; 164 M.Sobreira/Alamy Stock Photo; 165 Living4Media/Jansje Klazinga; 166 Living4Media/Jansje Klazinga; 167 t GAP Interiors/Costas Picadas; 167 b Arcaid/Alyson Smith; 168 l GAP Interiors/Costas Picadas; 168 r Living4Media/Jansje Klazinga; 169 Paul Massey/Suzy Hoodless designer; 170–171 Shutterstock/sootra; 172 GAP Interiors/Douglas Gibb; 173 l Shutterstock/Denny Lako; 173 r Living4Media/ Peter Ericsson; 174 Zara Home; 175 Zara Home; 176 Pixabay/Granada/SJTUK; 178 Living4Media/Radoslaw Wojnar; 179 Susi Bellamy (www.susi-bellamy.com), photography by Peter Atkinson Photography; 180 Living4Media/Vierucci Eustachi; 181 l Living4Media/José-Luis Hausmann; 181 r Arcaid/Richard Bryant; 182 l Metallic Moroccan Pouffes from Graham and Green, £150. Credit: Graham and Green (01225 418 200, www.grahamandgreen.co.uk); 182 r Getty Images/Eric Hernandez; 183 Arcaid/Richard Powers; 184 Mindthegap Jardin Sauvage wallpaper www.mindtheg.com; 187 Living4Media/Matteo Manduzio; 188 l Living4Media/View Pictures; 188 r Mindthegap Jardin Sauvage wallpaper (www.mindtheg.com); 189 l Arcaid/Michael Freeman; 189 r Arcaid/Richard Powers; 190 t Andreas von Einsiedel/Alamy Stock Photo; 190 b GAP Photos/Chris Tubbs – Interior Designer for Interiors; 191 GAP Photos/Julien Fernandez; 192 Mindthegap Statues Antique wallpaper www.mindtheg.com; 193 t GAP Photos/Bureaux; 193 b Photography: Mads Mogensen, styling: Martina Hunglinger & wallpaper: Deborah Bowness; 195 Arcaid/Historic England; 196 Living4Media/Anne-Catherine Scoffoni; 197 l Andreas von Einsiedel/Alamy Stock Photo; 197 r Wallcovering: Fromental – Custom Chinoiserie in Custom colourway.Photo: David Jensen; 198 l naygiarra/Stockimo/Alamy Stock Photo; 198 r Living4Media/Matteo Manduzio; 199 Watts of Westminster Ussé Chinoiserie; 200 Living4Media/Tom Meadow; 201 t Living4Media/Winfried Heinze; 201 b GAP Interiors/Costas Picadas; 203 Timorous Beasties/London Toile Red & Pink on Cream Wallpaper; 204 l Living4Media/Great Stock; 204 r Living4Media/Great Stock; 205 l Living4Media/Andreas von Einsiedel; 205 r Living4Media/Guy Bouchet; 206 Living4Media/Peter Ericsson; 207 GAP Interiors/Colin Poole; 208 Living4Media/Great Stock; 209 t GAP Interiors/Clive Nichols – ROQUELIN, LOIRE VALLEY, FRANCE; 209 b Living4Media/Oxana Afanasyeva; 210 Vessel wallpaper in British Lichen by Mini Moderns; 211 Tracy Kendall/Photographer Ollie Harrop; 212 l Andreas von Einsiedel/Alamy Stock Photo; 212 r Bespoke Kaleidoscope Wallpaper, made to order by Identity Papers; 213 Andreas von Einsiedel/Alamy Stock Photo; 214 Lucky Lantern wallpaper in Winter Plum by Mini Moderns; 215 t GAP Interiors/Douglas Gibb – Interior Designer Elina Helenius; 215 b GAP Interiors/Costas Picadas – Interior Designers Bob and Courtney Novogratz/The Turett Collaborative Architects; 216 Emma J Shipley 'Rousseau' cotton satin fabric for Clarke & Clarke; 218 Living4Media/Anne-Catherine Scoffoni; 219 Geometric Aviary wallpaper by Divine Savages www.divinesavages.com; 220 GAP Interiors/Sandra van Aalst; 221 l Daniel Heath Studio & Tom Fallon (photographer); 221 r Getty Images/Vostok; 222 l Living4Media/Great Stock; 222 r Alamy/Matilda Norris; 223 Living4Media/Stephani Buchman; 224–225 Interior design by Lisa Gilmore Design; photography: Seamus Payne; 226 GAP Interiors/Bureaux; 227 t GAP Photos/Costas Picadas; 227 b Living4Media/Eustachi Vierucci; 228 Living4Media/Catherine Gratwicke; 229 GAP Interiors/Costas Picadas; 230 l Living4Media/Content Agency; 230 r GAP Interiors/Costas Picadas; 231 l GAP Interiors/Douglas Gibb; 231 r GAP Interiors/Colin Poole; 232 Photography from Mark Alexander; 234 t Living4Media/Great Stock; 234 b Living4Media/Francesca Pagliai; 235 Fabrics by Mark Alexander, markalexander.com; 236 Fabrics by Mark Alexander, markalexander.com; 237 l Living4Media/Emotive Images; 237 r GAP Photos/Amanda Turner; 238 l Living4Media/Simon Maxwell Photography; 238 r Tracy Kendall/Photographer Ollie Harrop; 239 Portrait Communications/Jonathan Adler; 240 t GAP Interiors/John Downs; 240 b GAP Interiors/David Cleveland; 241 Rachel Dein/Joakim Blockstrom for Hide Restaurant; 242 Daniel Heath Studio & Tom Fallon (photographer); 243 Wallcovering: Fromental – Belize Tiles in colourway Burton. Photo: David Jensen; 244 Kirill Istomin/Photo by Stephan Julliard; 245 l Living4Media/Ines Kohnert; 245 r GAP Interiors/Caruth Studio; 246 GAP Interiors/Nick Smith; 247 t GAP Interiors/Nick Smith – Interior Design Wilding and Wolfe; 247 b GAP Interiors/Douglas Gibb – Interior Designer Colin Wong; 248 Natasha Baradaran (www.natashabaradaran.com)/Photographer: Roger Davies; 249 GAP Interiors/Hanna Dlugosz.